HOLIDAY CLUB
Programme
for 5- to 11-year olds

© Scripture Union 2014
First published 2014
ISBN 978 1 84427 840 4

Scripture Union
207–209 Queensway, Bletchley, Milton Keynes, MK2 2EB
Email: info@scriptureunion.org.uk
Website: www.scriptureunion.org.uk

British Library Cataloguing-in-Publication Data
A catalogue record of this book is available from the
British Library.

Printed in India by Nutech Print Services

Cover and internal design: kwgraphicdesign

Cover and internal illustrations: Sean Parks

Main contributor: Jenny Cheung

Additional material by Alex Taylor, Elise Allanson,
Sarah Bingham, Alice Langtree

Scripture Union is an international Christian charity
working with churches in more than 130 countries.

Thank you for purchasing this book. Any profits from
this book support SU in England and Wales to bring the
good news of Jesus Christ to children, young people
and families and to enable them to meet God through
the Bible and prayer.

Find out more about our work and how you can get
involved at:
- www.scriptureunion.org.uk (England and Wales)
- www.suscotland.org.uk (Scotland)
- www.suni.co.uk (Northern Ireland)
- www.scriptureunion.org (USA)
- www.su.org.au (Australia)

contents

INTRODUCTION

POLar EXPLOrers is a five- to seven-day children's holiday club: an opening service, three to five (daily) club sessions and a closing service.

With the help of **Sir Random Finds** and **Bare Feet**, the children are explorers who go on a mini-expedition each day and learn about a New Testament character. Through the lives of these people, they learn that no one is too *anything* to be part of God's big expedition, that is, to be a friend of Jesus and go out and help other people be friends of Jesus too.

GO2

What do you want to do next?

- For full details of the aims, theme, setting and roles of **POLar EXPLOrers**, go to pages 8–19.

- For general help and hints on running a holiday club, go to page 20.

- For outlines for each day's session, go to page 33.

- For a resource bank of activity ideas, go to page 70.

God's **big** expedition

Service 1
Never too hopeless…
Luke 24:13–34; Matthew 28:18–20

Expedition 1
Never too many mistakes…
Matthew 16:8; John 18:1–27; Acts 2

Expedition 2
Never too ordinary…
Acts 6

Expedition 3
Never too near or far…
Acts 8:26–39

Expedition 4
Never too bad…
Acts 9:1–31

Expedition 5
Never too young…
Acts 16; 1 Timothy 4; 2 Timothy 1

Service 2
Never too unlikely…
Acts 16:11–15

Never too … to be part of God's big expedition

Who is it for?

Every effort has been made to ensure that this programme is suitable for children with little or no church background. It is a tool for churches whose desire is to reach out to children and their families outside their church community. It should work equally well for churches wishing to use it as a discipleship resource for children already part of the church family.

Hints and tips are given with each day's session for children who are new to a faith-based club, who are used to church, who have additional needs and who have backgrounds from other faiths.

The POLar EXPLOrers resource book

Packed with creative ideas on how to explore stories from the New Testament about early Christians – ideas you can change and adapt to suit your club and context. There are also ideas for construction (craft), games, drama, creative prayer and worship. **POLar EXPLOrers** has a mixture of upfront presentation and small-group activities, allowing the children and leaders to build meaningful relationships with each other and with God.

The POLar EXPLOrers DVD

CBeebies presenter, Gemma Hunt, is trying to encourage the reluctant husky dog, Blizz, to join the sled team and be part of the polar expedition. Through stories of New Testament characters, beautifully illustrated by children's artist Ruth Hearson, she encourages his confidence to grow, and helps the children to see that they are never too *anything* to be part of God's big expedition.

The DVD also contains the **POLar EXPLOrers** song, backing tracks, training material for your team, administration forms and additional resources.

EXPEDITION LOG for 8 to 11s

This 48-page booklet contains all the key Bible text taken from the Contemporary English Version, along with small-group material, puzzles and extra information. It is ideal for use with 8 to 11s.

TraveL LOG for 5 to 8s

This 32-page booklet contains retold Bible stories, with key Bible verses taken from the Contemporary English Version, along with small-group material, puzzles and extra information, for younger children.

There are hints and tips for using both these resources as part of the small-group time in each day's Expedition. Both **EXPEDITION LOG** and **TraveL LOG** help maintain contact with children's homes and act as a reminder, in the weeks after the club, of what the children experienced at **POLar EXPLOrers**. You can buy **EXPEDITION LOG** or **TraveL LOG** as multiple copies – see the inside cover for details.

The POLar EXPLOrers website

Visit the **POLar EXPLOrers** website at **www.scriptureunion.org.uk/polarexplorers** for:

- printable versions of the photocopiable resources
- forms for club administration
- songs and sheet music
- logos, posters
- training sessions for your team
- ideas for involving families and friends of those at the club…

… and more!

You can also read about other people's experiences and check out the advice given by other users on the message boards.

The holiday club programme is written for the 5 to 11 age group. On the website you will also find:

- a parallel programme for under-5s, following the same Bible passages and themes as the main programme
- a parallel programme for 11 to 14s, following the same Bible passages and themes as the main programme
- a training course for young leaders aged 14 to 18 (Junior Huskies)

Once you have decided the best age group for your club, **POLar EXPLOrers** will have the activities to fit!

The **POLar EXPLOrers** theme song

The song 'Searching for your truth' is the **POLar EXPLOrers** holiday club theme song.

Song lyrics and sheet music are available on page 87 or the **POLar EXPLOrers** website or DVD. An MP3 of the song is also available to purchase from the Scripture Union online shop (www.scriptureunion.org.uk/shop).

Learn and remember song

'Speedy shoes' has been written to help the children learn the **POLar EXPLOrers** *Learn and remember* verse: Ephesians 6:15.

Song lyrics and sheet music are available on the **POLar EXPLOrers** website or DVD. An MP3 of the song is also available to purchase from the Scripture Union online shop (www.scriptureunion.org.uk/shop).

Training downloads and workshops

For training videos on topics such as 'Leading small groups', visit www.scriptureunion.org.uk/Shop/Multimedia (CDsDVDsVideodownloadsetc)/Videodownloads/Childrensandyouthworktraining videos/

There's also a training feature included on the **POLar EXPLOrers** DVD.

To plan and recruit your **POLar EXPLOrers** team, go to page 14.

For workshop sessions for training your team, go to the **POLar EXPLOrers** website.

Top Tips on Running holiday clubs

Practical advice and real-life experience to help you run a Bible-based holiday club, with suggestions to inspire and help you grow your team.

Publicity materials and merchandise

See the inside back cover for details of the publicity materials produced by Christian Publicity and Outreach. (Please note, CPO resources are not available through Scripture Union.)

Checklist

Which resources will you need to run your club and how many of each?

	Quantity
POLar EXPLOrers resource book	
POLar EXPLOrers DVD	
EXPeDITIOn LOG (8–11s)	
Single copy	
10-pack	
TraveL LOG (5–8s)	
Single copy	
10-pack	
Theme song MP3	
Learn and remember song MP3	
Training video downloads	
Top Tips on Running Holiday Clubs	

Remember to visit the **POLar EXPLOrers** website and download:

All documents as a zipfile	
Your choice of documents	

BASICS

BASICS 1

Aims and BIBLE Programme

What are *your* aims?

The aims of **Polar Explorers** are below, but each individual holiday club will have its own specific aims, too. **Polar Explorers** can provide a manageable, creative and fun way of reaching out to the children of your neighbourhood with the welcoming love of Jesus. It can provide an excellent opportunity to blow any misconceptions away about God and the Bible and show that following Jesus can be a great adventure.

You are likely to be focusing on the days or week of your club, but remember that the holiday club is not an isolated event. Where does it fit into your plans for children's work and with your church's ongoing evangelism and discipleship programme? How might you build on this to draw children further into church life (not necessarily or only through Sunday worship)? What opportunities will the club offer for your church to be more involved with the local community or to create and sustain links with schools in your area?

Working out your aims

- Make a copy of page 86 or print it from the **Polar Explorers** website.
- Cut the page into strips.
- Cut some blank strips as well.
- Get together with others, including your church leaders and holiday club team.
- Write your own aims on the blank strips.
- Mix all the strips together.

What do you want your holiday club to achieve, in *your* situation?

- As a group, sort the aims into *your* order of priority.
- Pick out the top aims (a maximum of three) and make sure all the team members know them.

Plan to evaluate **Polar Explorers** after the event to see if you met your aims.

- Decide now how you'll do that.
- How will you measure success?

Go to the **Polar Explorers** website www. scriptureunion.org.uk/polarexplorers to download a form to assess how you met your aims.

The aims of **Polar Explorers**

Through stories from the New Testament, **Polar Explorers** explores how the Holy Spirit changed people to change the world. These early Christians weren't too hopeless or too ordinary, they were never too *anything* to serve God. The Easter story forms the backdrop of this programme, giving ample opportunity for children to engage with the gospel while exploring the lives of some remarkable people, and encouraging them to be part of God's big expedition.

Aims

- To introduce the children to some characters from Acts and to see how they lived for Jesus, and the impact they had on the lives of those they met.
- To invite the children to be part of God's big expedition by becoming lifetime followers of Jesus, and to enable children who are already in a relationship with him to grow in their faith and understanding.
- To create lasting positive memories of Christian community, to build relationships and help children and their families become part of a church community.
- To offer a safe and fun environment for all the children.

- To encourage the growth of Christian faith in all the adults who are involved in the club, whether team members or parents/carers who may be on the premises for the very first time.

The POLar EXPLOrers Bible programme

The services begin with the Easter story and conclude with the story of Lydia. The message is that no one is too *anything* to become a follower of Jesus. Between these two worship events are the Bible stories of the club sessions, the Expeditions, featuring five different characters from the book of Acts.

Presenting the Bible story

The Bible story is told using the **POLar EXPLOrers** DVD, which has a story episode for each of the five Expeditions. Gemma Hunt and her husky dog puppet, Blizz, introduce the theme for each day. Gemma then tells the Bible story using cartoon artwork. Using the DVD allows the children to experience a different voice and setting, and the cartoon artwork brings the stories to life.

If you wish to tell the story as well as using the DVD, there are full scripts for reading aloud on the **POLar EXPLOrers** website. Or you may have a gifted storyteller on your team: encourage them to use their skills and bring the Bible passages to life, in their own way.

Bible references, storylines and aims: day by day

Service 1
Never too hopeless…

KEY PASSAGES
Luke 24:13–34, Matthew 28:18–20

KEY STORYLINES
- Jesus has been crucified and resurrected.
- He appears to his followers – specifically in the episode on the road to Emmaus.
- Jesus commissions his followers to be disciples who make disciples.

KEY AIMS
- To outline the events of Jesus' death and resurrection, and his great commission to his followers.
- To launch the holiday club so that church members know how to pray for it in the coming week(s).
- To welcome any children and their associated adults coming to the club who are not usually part of the worshipping community.

• •

Expedition 1
Never too many mistakes…

KEY CHARACTER AND PASSAGE
Peter – Matthew 16:18; John 18:1–27; Acts 2

KEY STORYLINES
- Peter was one of Jesus' closest friends and followers, but he made an awful lot of mistakes. When Jesus had been arrested, before he was crucified, Peter denied that he even knew Jesus.
- When the Holy Spirit came, Peter preached an amazing message to all the people, many came to know Jesus and the early church was formed.
- We need to have the right equipment/clothing for the expedition we are going on.

KEY AIMS
- To welcome the children and set the tone for the club.
- To help the children understand that however much we have messed up in the past, God can restore us and use us in ways we never dreamed of.
- To help the children begin to explore that we are never too *anything* for God to use us.
- To help children begin to understand the concept of Kingdom Footprints: how what we do with God leaves positive marks on the world around us.

• •

Expedition 2
Never too ordinary…

KEY CHARACTER AND PASSAGE
Stephen – Acts 6

KEY STORYLINES
- Stephen was chosen to help the apostles by organising the food.
- Although this didn't seem like a glamorous job, the Bible tells us that Stephen was full of the Holy Spirit, as well as grace and power and did many signs and wonders.
- We need to have the right provisions for the expedition we are going on.

KEY AIMS
- To welcome the children (back) to the club.
- To help the children understand that however unglamorous and in the background we feel, God will use us in amazing ways.
- To explore that God will give us his Holy Spirit to help us do whatever job he calls us to.
- To help the children discover Stephen's Kingdom Footprint.

Expedition 3
Never too near or far…

KEY CHARACTER AND PASSAGE
Philip – Acts 8:26–39

KEY STORYLINES
- Philip had a very successful ministry preaching God's Word in Samaria, but God called him away to travel on a desert road.
- Because of Philip's obedience, the Ethiopian came to know Jesus.
- We need to have a compass to show us where we are on our expedition.

KEY AIMS
- To welcome the children (back) to the club.
- To help the children understand that we can serve God wherever we are.
- To explore how Philip was ready to be used by God wherever he was.
- To help the children discover Philip's Kingdom Footprint.

Expedition 4
Never too bad…

KEY CHARACTER AND PASSAGE
Saul – Acts 9:1–31

KEY STORYLINES
- Saul had been one of the key enemies of Jesus and his followers – he'd even had Christians killed.
- Jesus met Saul on the road to Damascus; Saul spent the rest of his life following Jesus and sharing his good news.
- We need to have a map to help us navigate on our expedition.

KEY AIMS
- To welcome the children back to the club.
- To help the children understand that God doesn't let what we have been prevent us from being part of his big expedition.
- To help the children continue to explore that we are never too *anything* for God to use us. Today the children will see that God can turn any life around – even those who think they're beyond his reach.
- To help the children discover Saul's Kingdom Footprint.

Expedition 5
Never too young…

KEY CHARACTER AND PASSAGES
Timothy – Acts 16;1 Timothy 4; 2 Timothy 1

KEY STORYLINES
- Timothy was a young disciple who had been brought up by godly family.
- Timothy, despite his youth, had great character and was picked by two of the church's major players (Paul and Silas) to go on mission with them.
- We need to have a way of recording information to help us remember the key points from our expedition.

KEY AIMS
- To welcome the children to the club.
- To help the children understand that God doesn't let our young age get in the way of us being part of his big expedition.
- To explore Timothy's story and see how he worked for God.
- To help children uncover Timothy's Kingdom Footprint.

Service 2
Never too unlikely…

KEY CHARACTER AND PASSAGE
Lydia – Acts 16:11–15

KEY STORYLINES
- Paul, Silas, Timothy and Luke met Lydia on their journey in a city called Philippi.
- Lydia was important and wealthy – and also a woman – all of which might have made her an unlikely candidate for becoming a Christian.
- Lydia came to faith and because she was a community leader, many other people came to faith through her.

KEY AIMS
- To hear about many of the different characters who were part of God's big expedition.
- To share with the rest of the church community what's been happening at **POLar EXPLOrers**.
- To welcome any children and their associated adults who have been to the club wouldn't usually come to a service. The service needs to tread the line between being like the holiday club but also like a service.

A shorter holiday club programme

Not every group will want to run a holiday club for five sessions, so **POLar EXPLOrers** can also be run for three or four club days (in addition to the services). Icons at the top of each Expedition show which clubs to use it for. For example, an Expedition with just the '5' icon at the top is only for five-day clubs, while one with the '3', '4' and '5' icons is for three, four and five-day clubs. A paragraph at the beginning of each Expedition suggests any adaptations shorter clubs should make.

GO2

What do you want to do next?
- For details of the theme, setting and team roles, read on.
- To plan what needs to be done and when, go to page 30.
- For the daily sessions (Expeditions) go to page 33.

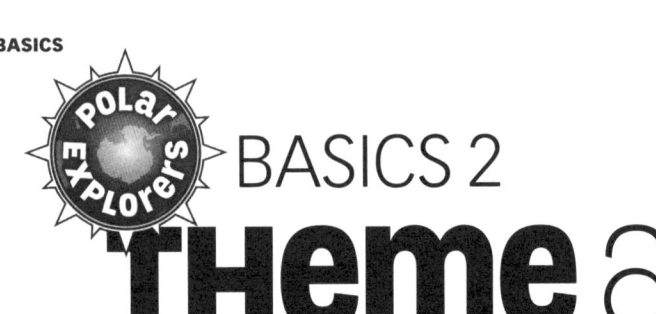

BASICS 2
Theme and SETTING

All about POLar EXPLORers

The scene is a polar exploration base camp, which could be either the North or South Pole, or a fictional pole. The session material will work with any of these. If you decide to choose a specific pole, remember in your theming of the club and the meeting space that the North Pole has igloos and polar bears, and the South Pole has penguins!

The setting leads into the idea of Bible exploration: the holiday club is about helping children explore the lives of New Testament characters and understand that they are never too *anything* to be part of God's big expedition: to be a friend of Jesus and go out to help other people start being friends of Jesus too.

Characters in POLar EXPLORers

These personality profiles describe the characters as they are presented in the Expedition material. You are, of course, free to change and adapt the characters to suit your club and fit the members of your team.

Sir Random Finds is a seasoned explorer who knows all about how to go on an expedition, but nothing about carbon footprints. He helps Bare Feet to understand all the different things that will help her when she goes out exploring. In parallel, he introduces the children to the Bible characters they are going to explore and helps them to understand that they, too, can be part of God's big expedition.

Bare Feet has come to study the carbon footprint. However, she knows nothing about polar exploration, so Sir Random Finds helps her each day as she sets out on her expeditions. She also introduces the children to the idea of a Kingdom Footprint, the special footprint that we can leave on the world around us when we show other people what God is like.

Explorers are the children at **POLar EXPLORers**. Each day they go on a mini expedition in which they find out about a New Testament character and learn that they are never too *anything* to be part of God's big expedition.

Teams are the small groups of explorers that the children are part of throughout the club. The children will gather in their team HQ at the start of the day, and then go there to explore the Bible, have their refreshments, pray together and do games and construction.

How many children and age groups you have in your teams will vary from club to club. Some points to consider, including child to adult ratios, are given in the registration coordinator's role description on page 17.

Each team is led by a Husky, who may be helped by one or more Junior Huskies.

Setting up your venue

The best place to meet

Choosing the right venue is very important. Sometimes a community hall or school is a well-equipped, neutral venue that can be non-threatening for children and parents outside the church. However, you may wish to use this opportunity to introduce children and parents to your church building. This can also help save on the cost of hiring an alternative venue. The venue needs to have enough space for the number of children and the types of activities you are planning. You will need access to the venue before the holiday club to ensure necessary preparations can be made.

Setting up the room

If you have the space and can leave your room set up, from day to day, there are many ways to transform your club space into a polar expedition base. Members of the congregation may well be able to lend skis, ski clothes and other winter sports equipment. Fake snow of various types can be bought online all year round (do a web search on 'fake snow' to see the range of things on offer). Experiment with a projector (even an old overhead one) to project photos of snowflakes or polar scenes on the walls or floor, especially as children arrive for the club. You can find amazing photos on sites such as Pinterest.

All this will help to spark the children's imaginations. Think creatively about how you can transform your venue into an exciting place.

If you cannot leave your room set up from day to day, prepare pictures on display boards or large banners which can be put into place quickly at the start of each session. Make sure you allow extra time for this and have team members lined up to help.

Fill the screen
If you are using a video projector or OHP to project the song words, for example, use interesting images when it is not being used, so that the screen is never blank. Find the **Polar Explorers** logo and other themed artwork on the DVD-ROM section of the **Polar Explorers** DVD or at the **Polar Explorers** website).

Extra rooms
If you have more than one room, think carefully about which activities to site in which part of the venue. You need easy routes between rooms and to minimise 'shuffle time' between different parts of your timetable.

If you have multiple rooms, appoint someone (maybe a Junior Husky) to be the 'explorer guide' each day. This person will remind groups in distant venues about the time, take messages for Sir Random Finds and generally help get everyone to the right place at the right time.

Venue maps
Once you have decided the locations within your venue, give each team member a map to remind them of what is happening where – and so that they can work out where they need to be at any given time in the session. Include emergency exits, toilets and 'no entry' areas on the map, too.

Spaces, within the venue

Upfront presentation
The holiday club will be greatly enhanced if the area (a stage, if possible) where the up-front presentation takes place can be transformed into a polar expedition base camp. This is where Sir Random Finds and Bare Feet will run the programme. The boundary for the stage area can be marked by a masking tape line across the floor.

Drama
Think about where you will present the daily drama. This is probably not your main presentation area as the scenery will need to change for each drama episode (details are given with the drama scripts on pages 77 to 85 in the Expedition Store). A raised stage is ideal to allow all the children to see the action.

Band
Position Poles Apart carefully; they are likely to come with large amounts of equipment and need access to electricity. Leave space for the stage to be used for other things, too! Keep the children away from this area and make sure that routes around the building do not require them to step over cables, and so on.

Screen(s) and projector
Work out where to locate the projection screen, for projecting song words, club logo and so on; and where to position the projector so it does not obstruct the children's view or become a hazard.

'Green room'
A draped-off area or a linking room will be useful for the drama team to emerge from. This can double as a 'staff room' for team members.

Team HQs
The rest of the room can be divided into an HQ for each team. Remember, each team will include adult Huskies and six to eight children, both explorers and Junior Huskies. Make sure you have allowed enough space in each HQ for this number of people, and enough space overall for the number of teams you are going to need.

Much will depend on whether the areas can be left from day to day. Larger space could mean the HQs can become more elaborate as the week progresses, with banners and flags, collections of things the children have found or made and areas for sitting and working.

If there is only room for a table and chairs, aim to decorate all wall space or dividers to make the team HQ as distinctly unique as possible.

Is everyone going to sit on the floor for most of the time together in the team? If so, provide mats and cushions to sit on and clipboards for them to lean on.

BASICS 3
Team roles and Tasks

Don't panic! You are not going to need a team of fifty people to run your club (though that would be nice…)! Happy clubs run with two or three adults and a handful of children; other clubs have a large team and two hundred children – and are just as happy!

These pages will take you through all the roles and functions that will help your club run smoothly. Not all have to happen at the holiday club or all the time the club is running, so individuals may take on several roles and functions.

The holiday club (and those taking part) will thrive when there are a variety of support teams and when individuals take responsibility for different areas of the programme. If you are running a holiday club for the first time and only have a small team of volunteers you may not be able to fill all these roles or teams. So, we have noted which roles we see as essential (indicating some extra tasks those people will need to take on) and those that are great to have, if you are blessed with a larger team.

Possible roles are listed in the table on page 15 with space for you to write in the name(s) of the team members. Remember that these are the roles, the different tasks that people may do. You do not need a different person for each role – and many roles are optional, the club will still work without them. Team roles and tasks are explained in more detail on pages 16–19.

Job descriptions for each role are also available at the **POLar EXPLOrers** website.

Print these out for each person on the team to help everyone know how they fit into the whole club. (Some people may have several job descriptions.) Use the reverse side of the sheet to remind them of specific details of your holiday club, such as dates, times, your club aims, training workshops and so on.

It is possible (though very hard work!) to run a holiday club with a minimum team of three adult leaders. The larger and more experienced your team, the more options and activities you can offer, but don't be put off by small numbers. Work and adapt with what you've got.

Team roles and functions: in summary

The table on page 15 shows all the roles you may choose to use in your holiday club: some are optional and others can be combined.

Team roles and functions: in detail

Club leader
The overall leader and coordinator is ideally someone who is not involved in the presentation. Their role is to:
- lead the planning of the holiday club, before and during the event
- make any on-the-spot decisions, such as accepting extra children at the door
- keep the whole programme to time, moving things on when necessary
- look at quality of presentation, watching out for problems such as too much drifting off the timetable
- watch out for children who are not joining in well and help them to become part of things
- be the person to whom everyone would report in the event of a fire
- liaise with parents and carers; be a PR figure.

3 TEAM ROLES AND TASKS

Team roles and functions

Role	Function	Essential optional	Upfront/behind the scenes	Special skills	Team member
Club leader	Overall leader of the holiday club	Essential	Behind the scenes	Organisation, monitoring, leading	
Core planning team	Small group to lead organising the club	Essential	Behind the scenes	Organisation	
Sir Random Finds	Co-presenter (main)	Essential	Upfront	Confident, able to engage and involve children	
Bare Feet	Co-presenter (main)	Essential	Upfront	Confident, able to engage and involve children	
Huskies	Small group leaders	Essential	A bit of both	Leading small groups of children	
Junior Huskies	Junior leaders or helpers	Optional	A bit of both	Willing to learn and join in	
Registration coordinator and team	Books children in; keeps records	Essential	Both	Attention to detail, welcoming and friendly	
Poles Apart	Live worship band	Optional	Upfront	Musical; leading worship	
Drama leader	Recruits drama team; runs daily drama	Optional	Both	Acting and team leading	
Games coordinator	Organises all games activities at the club	Optional	Either or both	Energy and enthusiasm	
Construction/craft organiser	Organises hands-on creative activities	Optional	Either or both	Creativity and patience	
Refreshment person or team	Makes sure refreshments happen on time and safely	Essential	Behind the scenes	Organisation and planning	
First-aider	As required; maintains records	Preferable	Behind the scenes	Current first aid qualification	
Technical manager	Makes sure everything works as and when it should	Optional, depending on what you are using	Behind the scenes	Practical and technical	
Photographer	Takes photographs throughout the club	Optional	Both	Good at photographing children without disturbing their activities	
Publicity and admin person or team	Publicises the club; club paperwork	Optional	Behind the scenes		
Health and safety person	Ensures safety of everyone at the club	Optional	Behind the scenes	Risk assessments	
Meeters and greeters	Available to chat to adults as they bring and collect their children	Optional, but particularly useful on the first day	A bit of both	Welcoming, friendly and reassuring	
Prayer team	Prays	Essential	Behind the scenes		

Core planning team

All the helpers should be involved in planning and preparing for **POLAR EXPLORERS**, but you will need a smaller team to coordinate things and make some initial decisions. As well as the holiday club's overall leader, this should include your most experienced leaders, your minister and your children's workers.

Sir Random Finds and Bare Feet: the main upfront presenters

The main presenters of **POLAR EXPLORERS**. Together, they guide children through each session, introducing the different elements and delivering some of the teaching for the day.

They should be confident in their roles upfront and have experience of leading a programme in a fun but flexible manner. They need to keep the programme moving and engage with the children.

Huskies and Junior Huskies

These are the leaders of each expedition team (small group) and those helping them. The Husky has responsibility for the explorers (children) in the expedition team and will also be supporting the Junior Huskies, who may never have been involved in a holiday club before or may be someone who could be a leader at next year's club.

Huskies

The small group Husky should be at the club every day and will be the person with whom the children have the most personal contact. The leader's role is to get to know the children so that they feel welcome and comfortable at **POLAR EXPLORERS**. The programme is designed to give these leaders enough time in their teams and at their team HQ to have meaningful discussions, including ones that apply the teaching programme to the children's lives.

They should coordinate all small-group activities and sit with the children in their expedition teams during the upfront times. They should have a copy of the register and be aware of any special needs and food allergies, ensuring that children all leave safely at the end of the day's session.

If you have a large holiday club, you may appoint someone to coordinate six or eight expedition teams who are all in one age range. It is best if these coordinators do not have a group of their own.

Junior Huskies

The role of the Junior Husky is to support the Husky, and ideally they should also be available every day. This is a good way to develop the leadership skills of young or inexperienced team members.

Huskies and Junior Huskies could wear expedition-type clothes, such as walking boots and walking trousers, or even ski equipment. However, the clothes need to also be practical for the likely temperature during your club.

For training materials for use specifically with 14 to 18s in leadership, go to the **POLAR EXPLORERS** website.

Under-18s count as children, when you're working out adult:child ratios. If you have a lot of Junior Huskies, you will need *more* Huskies, rather than fewer.

All team members should be given training in dealing with children, especially in relation to physical contact and not being with children alone out of sight of others, but Huskies and Junior Huskies especially need to be aware of child protection issues and policies.

think about

New to running a holiday club? Or new team members this time?

More experienced but wanting to work on aspects like storytelling or leading small groups?

Even if your team members already work with children in the church, the shared experience of training together will benefit all of you!

Go to the **POLAR EXPLORERS** website for training modules on a whole range of topics and skills that will build your confidence as leaders.

Registration coordinator (and team)

Responsible for:

- allocating of children to expedition teams
- checking children in and out each day
- checking forms are completed fully
- making a register, based on names and ages
- giving a copy of the register to the Husky of each expedition team
- keeping a check on team sizes if more children register during **POLar EXPLOrers**
- ensuring each child is to be picked up or has permission to walk home themselves. If you have a lot of children attending the club, it can be hard to keep track of who has permission to collect which child, especially when parents help each other out. A collection slip, which can be given to the adult who will pick the child up, is on the **POLar EXPLOrers** website.

Forward planning

If possible, encourage parents of children to complete booking forms in advance, to be returned to the leader of the holiday club, school office or community group leader. This means you can allocate children to groups in advance and will already be aware of dietary requirements, medical issues and physical, educational or behavioural special needs. Remember to check these when planning the club activities!

'On the day' registration

In some contexts, pre-registering is not practical: ensure on the first day that there are plenty of extra volunteers available to help greet the children and their parents or carers and to provide them with the registration form to fill in. Children should not attend the event if permission has not been granted. As this can be a lengthy process, you should open the doors earlier on the first day. If the registration process is extended, engage the children in parachute games, upfront games or a short film.

Identification

- Each team member should have an appropriate, clearly labelled badge to identify them and their role.
- The children registered for **POLar EXPLOrers** should each have their own badge which should be taken off before they leave the club.
- Any adult or child on site not wearing an appropriate badge should be challenged.

Each child can be given a new sticky-backed badge each day, when they register.

Parents may not like their children to wear pin badges since they can be sharp and can damage clothes.

Creating teams

Size and makeup of teams will vary from club to club, but need to be given careful consideration. Each team should be small enough for the group leaders to get to know the individual children very quickly and also small enough to enable a group discussion to take place. Adult:child ratios are very important; check the **POLar EXPLOrers** website for specific guidance and remember that junior leaders count as children when working out ratios.

Some things to think about for your club:

- Will you sort the groups by age?
- What will you do if siblings or friends want to stay together but don't match your categories?
- Will you have boys' groups and girls' groups or mixed gender? What could be the benefits of each?
- Do you have space for the number of groups you are planning?
- Do you have enough adult leaders for the number of groups you are planning? (Remember the ratios: you can't keep increasing the size of the group!)
- How will you integrate children who join the club later in the week?

Poles Apart

Having a live band can add something special to a holiday club. The band could be creatively dressed to show elements from the two different Poles, for example, penguins and polar bears. If you can't use live music, then sing along to a CD. You could also consider having a group of dancers instead, who lead everyone in actions to songs, either with existing actions or their own.

Drama leader (and team)

The drama team needs a leader to recruit a team of five to ten actors who are reasonably confident and have the ability to project their voices, and coordinate rehearsals. They should appoint one of the drama team to collect and prepare any costumes and props. The drama team should be willing to learn their lines and to practise each sketch until they can perform it with confidence.

Games coordinator

This person needs to:

- consider what games to play, based on the number of children, your venue and equipment available
- take responsibility for ensuring all the games equipment is in the correct place at the right time
- plan for bad-weather alternatives, if you are hoping to be outside for games
- explain how to play each game
- supervise the activity, if required.

Construction/craft organiser

This person needs to:

- acquire materials and equipment beforehand (ask people for specific items, go shopping, visit a local scrapstore)
- take responsibility for ensuring all the equipment needed for the construction is in the correct places at the right time
- get as much as possible of the craft preparations done in advance (there may well be church members who can't help at the club but will be happy to help with cutting out, shopping and so on)

Think about

A group of people to source the necessary materials will be invaluable, especially in the run-up to **POLar EXPLorers**. They can make templates and patterns for the children to draw around or cut out, help produce prototypes of each design and pass on any hints to the Huskies.

Involve local schools in amassing reusable material to use during the week (such as yogurt pots, glass jars, plastic bottles, travel magazines for collage). This actively involves people in contributing to the club before it has begun, including the children, and alerts the school to the club's existence, bringing extra publicity.

- prepare a finished version of each item to show the children what they are making
- be able to explain how the item is made.

Refreshment person or team

This person and team will play a vital role during the club times. They will be responsible for:

- checking with the registration team that you have no children with food allergies
- obtaining and preparing the refreshments for the children at the agreed time
- being sensitive to faith-related food laws
- tidying up after the refreshments have been given out.

If you are providing anything more than a drink and a biscuit, you should have someone with a food hygiene certificate. Think about using (recyclable) disposable cups or bottles to save on washing-up time.

First-aider

Aim to have at least one member of your team with a valid first-aid certificate. If possible have assistants too – a male for the boys and a female for the girls. These people will need a current first aid certificate and access to a first aid kit. You will also need an accident book to record any incidents or accidents. (This is essential in the event of any insurance claim. A record of the matter should be noted, along with details of action taken. It should be countersigned where appropriate.)

Technical manager

The amount of technology used will vary with the size and nature of each club, but these days it is hard to manage without some technical equipment. A technical manager could take responsibility for setting-up and running:

- Visual – laptop and projector, or OHP; screen, or DVD and TV.
- Audio – PA for presenters and band, CD/MP3 player.

Photographer

Takes photographs throughout each expedition, to be used during *Into the unknown* in Expedition 5.

It is very important that the registration form includes permission to photograph each child, and that the photographer is clearly aware of any children who may not be photographed.

Publicity and club admin person or team

A computer-literate person, or team of people, should take responsibility for all the design, printing and publicity for **POLar EXPLOrers**. Your aim should be to produce publicity that is visually impressive, consistent, accurate and attractive.

For more ideas about publicity and club administration paperwork, before, during and after **POLar EXPLOrers**, go to page 26.

Health and safety person

The person in charge of health and safety will be responsible for ensuring that no child leaves the building unless they have permission to do so, and that only children or adults who are part of **POLar EXPLOrers** are allowed to enter the building or area set aside for the club.

Duties and responsibilites of the health and safety person are listed further in Basics 5: Legal requirements on page 29.

Meeters and greeters

It's not essential, but it can be a real bonus to have people 'hanging around' to chat with adults, as they bring or collect their children. You might like to invite church staff to be part of this informal team, especially if they are not helping to run the club: it is a good opportunity to start getting to know people. It is particularly useful to have extra helpers on the first day.

Prayer team

Make sure you have a team of people committed to pray throughout the preparation and the club itself. Keep the whole church well informed too. Again, this is something that church members who are not able to attend the club could be involved with.

The prayer team should keep on praying for the children in the club in the months after **POLar EXPLOrers**.

Developing people's potential

As well as being a time of great fun and development for the children attending, a holiday club is also an important time for the adults leading and helping out. Helping with a holiday club can be a big step for people in the development of their gifts and ministry.

How does a holiday club develop people's potential?

- It involves people in the church who don't usually work with children.
- It is an opportunity for people of all ages to work together in a way that may not happen at any other time of the year. (A regular comment at one holiday club from team members is, 'This is the best week of the year in church!' It's probably the most demanding and tiring too!)
- It discovers people's untapped gifts and enthusiasms.
- It develops people's gifts and lets them take risks.
- It provides a structure for the overall leadership of the club or church to seek out and encourage people to 'have a go'. Look at who you have available and ask people personally, giving them good reasons why you think they could fulfil whatever task you have identified. This suggests that you believe in them and they are far more likely to agree to get involved!

BASICS 4
PLANNING your programme

Services

POLaR EXPLoRERS includes two services for all-age worship, one to start the club and one to finish. These are designed to be an integral part of the club. As an opener for the club, the first service will have a clear aim and motivate children to want to attend. (Children who don't attend this first service will still find it easy to join the club on the first day, though!)

These give you a natural connection to encourage children from outside your church community and their families into a church service. Research shows that if you advertise the club as including the services (so a seven-day programme rather than a five-day one), children and families with little or no church background are more likely to attend.

The services could be at the same time as your usual Sunday service, or on a different day or at a different time.

GO2

- The all-age service for the start of the holiday club is on page 34.
- The all-age service for the end of the holiday club is on page 66.

Expeditions

The daily Expeditions in **POLaR EXPLoRERS** follow a regular pattern that has been popular with many groups, but you don't have to follow this pattern! Plan *your* programme for *your* club!

- Decide on the mix of 'all together' and 'small group' times that will work well with your venue, timing and numbers.
- Select which programme elements (more about these, below) are most important for you: put those into your programme first.
- Fit other activities around these core essentials.
- Arrange at least one training-and-preparation session for your team before the club. The **POLaR EXPLoRERS** DVD has a training module for you to use.
- Choose activities to bring out the best in your team: bear in mind their skills and experience.
- Select the activities according to the children you are likely to have at the club: they should be the most important consideration.
- Children respond differently to the same activity. (Huskies in particular should bear this in mind when planning activities for their expedition teams.)
- If you have a long club, then you will be able to do more! The timings given are merely guidelines; different children will take different lengths of time to complete the same activity.
- Be flexible in your timings, judge whether it would be more valuable to complete an activity, even though it may be overrunning, rather than cut it short and go on to the next activity.
- Have something in your programme you can drop if things overrun.

And why not extend your holiday club with events and activities to involve families and friends? Find ideas on pages 94–96.

Small group time (Expedition time)

Part of 'Expedition time' is likely to be spent in construction and games: suitable activities are in the Expedition Store. There are two popular ways to run these: chat with your team about what will work well for *your* club.

1 Every expedition team does the same game or activity on the same day. This requires a lot of resources and may limit the type of activity you use. It is easy to theme the activity closely with the Bible learning.

2 Certain activities are set up every day and the expedition teams rotate around them. This needs fewer resources and an extra leader can run the activity, while the Huskies have more time to interact with their expedition team; but your venue may not be large enough.

Programme elements:
in summary

Programme elements are listed on the table on page 22: the Expeditions, starting on page 38, give you activity material for each of these elements, every day of the club. Tick the ones you plan to use for your club – and remember, you can rearrange them in your own order. (We've put in a few ticks to start you off.)

These programme elements are described in more detail on pages 21–24.

For a two-hour club session, a popular timetable has a few minutes in small groups while everyone arrives; followed by a 45 minute 'all-together' time; the children then do activities in small groups for another 45 minutes; then come back together for a 20-minute all-together finish.

Programme elements:
in detail

Husky time: team preparation

Before the children arrive, have a short and focused team meeting. Each Expedition gives: a brief reflection on the Bible story of the day, prompts for prayer and practical reminders to make sure everything is as ready as it can be before the children arrive.

Sign up: Registration

The first moments at **POLar EXPLOrers** are so important! Be welcoming, but not overwhelming, to assure parents that their children will be safe with you while also giving the children a sense of the fun that they'll be having.

- Have enough people at the registration desk (especially on the first day) to show the children and their parents to the right groups.
- Make sure that the registration desk is well organised, with spare forms and pens for any parents who want to register their children at the door.
- Have a floor plan of your venue to show where each team is sited, so that parents can find their way round.
- Ideally, display a large plan nearby so that parents bringing several children can check, without clogging up the registration area.
- Ensure parents have filled in a collection slip so you know who will be picking the child up at the end of the session. Collection slips and registration forms are available at the **POLar EXPLOrers** website.
- Before the children go into the club, check they are wearing a name badge.

Do you copy?
Settling in and building relationships

While children are arriving, this is an important time for relationship building in individual teams.

- There are suggestions for ways for each team to customise their own team HQ on page 13.
- As the week goes on, team duties can include practising the *Learn and remember* verse, chatting about the Bible story from previous days and sharing news.
- Any child with jokes, pictures, messages or questions should place them in the *Uploaded data stream* as they arrive.

Base camp: all together for opening session

Bring everyone together for a fast-moving and fun opening session. This is led from the front and contains the main biblical teaching for the day's quest.

Situation report: welcome

Sir Random Finds and Bare feet introduce themselves and welcome everyone to the club. Sir Random Finds reminds everyone what God's big expedition is, and explains which New Testament character is the focus of today's expedition.

Programme elements

Title	What it is	Time (approx)	Children	Team	Tick
Husky time	Team preparation	30 minutes		Whole team	✓
Sign up	Registration		Individually	Registration team	✓
Do you copy?	Settling in; building relationships	10 minutes	Small groups	Huskies and Junior Huskies	
Base camp		45 minutes	Everyone together	Sir Random Finds and Bare Feet	✓
Situation report	Welcome			Sir Random Finds and Bare Feet	
Basic training	Daily challenge			Huskies	
Data report	Introduce today's theme			Sir Random Finds and Bare Feet	
Dancing on ice	Theme song and more			Poles Apart	
Message from base	Introduce the Bible story			Sir Random Finds	
Adventure tales	Bible storytelling			DVD	✓
Key data	Review today's teaching			Sir Random Finds	
Hear from the Husky	Interview a team member				
Learn and remember	*Learn and remember* verse				
Expedition time		45 minutes	Small groups	Huskies and Junior Huskies	
Refuelling station	Refreshments			Refreshment team	✓
Bible exploration	Bible discovery			Huskies	✓
Radio transmission	Prayer			Huskies	✓
Construction	Construction/craft			Huskies	
Games	Games			Huskies	
Expedition debrief		20 minutes	Everyone together	Sir Random Finds and Bare Feet	
Reporting back	Each team reports back			Sir Random Finds	
Uploaded data stream	Postbox				
Dancing on ice	Theme song and more			Poles Apart	
The Ice Adventure	Drama			Drama team	
Radio scan	Praying together			Sir Random Finds and Bare Feet	
Into the unknown	Extra all-together activity			Sir Random Finds	
Data upload	Finale			Sir Random Finds	✓
Over and out	Waiting to go	10 minutes	Small groups	Huskies and Junior Huskies	
Husky situation report	Clear up; debrief	30 minutes		Whole team	✓

Basic training: daily challenge
Each day, two leaders or children race to dress up in explorer's clothes. During the course of the club, a leader board records the times taken by each person.

Data report
Sir Random Finds and Bare feet introduce the theme for the day by talking about the different things Bare Feet needs to go on her expeditions.

Dancing on ice: **Polar Explorers** theme song
– and more!

It's great to have a number of musicians playing a variety of instruments, but if this is not feasible, use backing tracks or simply sing along to a CD or MP3.

- Choose and practise the songs beforehand.
- Mix new songs and a few old favourites, including songs about God and faith, so that children are not singing words they might not believe.
- Sing the **Polar Explorers** theme song every day, in the opening session and finale.

Message from base

Sir Random Finds sets the scene for the Bible story with a brief story of his own.

Adventure tales: Bible storytelling

This is the main storytelling section of the club. Each day's Bible story is on the **Polar Explorers** DVD; storytelling scripts are also available on the **Polar Explorers** website.

Key data

Sir Random Finds helps the children to think about today's story using the 'Never too…' phrase.

Hear from the Husky

One of the team leaders tells a personal story showing the difference today's teaching has made in their life.

Learn and remember: *learn and remember* verse

'Wear shoes that are able to speed you on as you preach the good news of peace with God' Ephesians 6:15 (*Living Bible*).

Each Expedition will suggest a way of memorising this verse, and a few words to help children understand the meaning of the verse as well as being able to recite it.

- The *Learn and remember* verse song (lyrics and score) is on the **Polar Explorers** website.
- The theme song (lyrics and score) is on page 87.
- MP3 files of both songs are on the DVD and available to purchase separately: see the **Polar Explorers** website.

think ab out

Are you planning to reward children or groups of children who demonstrate that they have learnt the verse?

When else might you give the children a reward?

There's also a song, 'Speedy shoes', on the **Polar Explorers** website and on the **Polar Explorers** DVD to help the children to learn the verse.

Expedition time: time spent in teams

The children move to their teams for Bible exploration, construction, games and refreshments. Encourage team members to see this time as an opportunity to build positive relationships with the children.

Refuelling station: refreshments

Make sure you have refreshments that are suitable for children of other faiths. The easiest way to do this is to provide food suitable for vegetarians (no gelatine) and which contains no pork products. Do tell everyone that the food is OK otherwise they might assume it isn't and not have any.

Bible exploration: Bible discovery

The Huskies help the children to explore the story in the Bible using the **EXPEDITION LOG** (8–11s) or the **Travel LOG** (5–8s).

Polar Explorers helps children explore and read the Bible for themselves. So each day in *Bible discovery* help the children to find the story in the Bible or in their booklets and learn to look for answers there. Use a translation that is easy for children to read (Good News Bible, Contemporary English Version, New Century Version or International Children's Bible).

It is important that Huskies have prepared for this key part of the programme, where the children have explicit opportunities to respond to God. The leaders' notes for each Expedition are also available to download from the **Polar Explorers** website.

Radio transmission: praying in small groups

Each day, there is a suggestion for how the **POLar EXPLOrers** might talk with God. Encourage every child to join in, whether silently or out loud.

Construction: craft

There are two types of construction: **POLar EXPLOrer** constructions that follow the theme of the club and can be done on any day, and Bible constructions that link with each Expedition's Bible teaching.

Whichever projects you choose to do, the construction time creates an environment where you can strengthen relationships, chat about the day's teaching and have fun together. The construction projects can be found in the Expedition store on pages 70 to 73, or for further inspiration, see *Ultimate Craft*.

Games

The games time is another good opportunity for leaders and children to chat, build relationships and to demonstrate biblical values in the way the games are played.

Games used during **POLar EXPLOrers** can be found on pages 74–76. For further inspiration, see *Ultimate Games*, which contains hundreds of ideas that might be suitable for your club. Make sure you risk-assess these activities and collect all the necessary materials beforehand.

Expedition debrief: all together again for the closing session

During this time, the children are all together for another session of activities, led from the front.

Reporting back

Each team has the opportunity to feed back to everyone their discovery of the day's Kingdom Footprint.

Uploaded data stream: postbox

This is essentially the club postbox, where the children post jokes, pictures, letters and anything else they would like to share. Depending on the amount of time you have, some or all of these can be read out or shown

Decorate your box to fit in with the theme of the club – maybe as a computer, a telex machine or a radio.

Dancing on ice: **POLar EXPLOrers** theme song – and more!

Poles Apart lead the children in a couple of lively songs.

The Ice Adventure: drama

The Ice Adventure is the story of four adventurers battling through the polar wastes with a vital message for the scientist Yvonne Von Evian, stationed beyond the snow plains, across the glacier and around the mountain. Each episode reflects the 'Never too…' message of that day's Expedition.

Radio scan: praying together

Each Expedition will give suggestions for encouraging your Huskies and **POLar EXPLOrers** to talk with God together, as they move towards a positive ending to the day.

Into the unknown:

A short, fun activity that reinforces the day's teaching.

Data upload: finale

This wraps up the all-together time. Summarise the main points of the story and remind the children of today's *Key data*. Tell the children what might be happening the next session to whet their appetites and remind them about the procedure for being collected by parents and carers.

Over and out: back to team HQs

This is a winding-down time while waiting to be collected when you can:
- use the activity suggestion in each Expedition
- finish off anything from the day's activities
- make sure the children have everything they need to take with them
- say goodbye and encourage the children to come again next time
- chat with those collecting their children.

Husky situation report: clearing up and a quick debrief

It may be that some of the team have their own children at **POLar EXPLOrers** and are unable to stay for long when the programme ends. Try to call everyone together to check any problems, briefly reminding them of the next session's activities and pray for the Holy Spirit to be at work in the children.

If you have time and the facilities, the team could share lunch together to round off the day.

BASICS 5
NUTS and BOLTS

Who, where and when

Who will you invite to POLAR EXPLOrers?

Look at the list of aims you drew up (page 8). Do your aims relate to

- the children already involved in your church?
  - those outside it?
  - both?

    Write your decision in the box below.

How many children do you want to involve?

If your main aim is to get to know the children better, you might need to restrict numbers. On the other hand, if you want to present the gospel to children who haven't heard it, you may want as many as possible to attend. The number of leaders you have will affect your child capacity in order to meet the required adult:child ratio. You may also have limits imposed by the size of your venue.

What age range(s) do you want to target with POLAR EXPLORers?

- Do you want to cater for an age range that is already well-represented in your groups, or one that isn't?
- Will you and your team be able to tailor the activities in a way that will appeal to a wide age range? Or will you target a narrower age range?
  - What training would help your team?

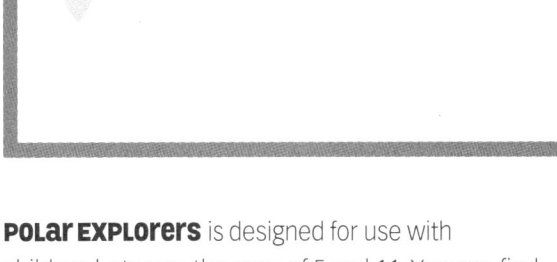

POLAR EXPLOrers is designed for use with children between the ages of 5 and 11. You can find parallel programmes for Under-5s and 11 to 14s at the **POLAR EXPLOrers** website.

Where and when?

If you run a holiday club regularly, you may already know when and where you will be meeting.

Any club needs to fix the date for early enough for people to take it into account when they book their holidays: this affects potential leaders' availability and also children who want to attend. It is not unusual for families to plan their holidays around a church club date!

Think about potential clashes with:
- other holiday clubs in the area
- activities already booked at your premises
- holidays and events organised by local schools
- holidays or camps for local Boys' Brigade, Girls' Brigade, Cub or Brownie groups carnivals or local events.

Or look at this another way and see if there is a way you can – intentionally – tie in your club with these events and benefit from the buzz around the local area.

Are other local churches running holiday clubs? Could you work together to maximise the impact in your area?
- Run one big club?
- Coordinate a sequence of clubs, on different dates with different programmes?
- Share publicity?

Time of year?

The summer break is the most obvious and popular time to hold your club. The potential leaders' availability will have the most effect on the duration of your holiday club. If most of your leaders need to take time off work, it may not be practical to run a full five-day club. Consider also:

- running the club in a half-term holiday or the Easter holidays
- holding the club on Sundays through the holiday period, if your other sessions stop running
  - running the club on the same day of the week, through the holiday period.

Length of session
- Will you run your club just in the morning or just in the afternoon? For a longer day?
  - Will you include evening sessions for whole families or extra 'fun days' at the weekends?

Publicity and club admin

Ensure plenty of children at your holiday club through effective use of publicity and promotional materials. Plan this as carefully as other aspects of your club; it's easy to spend a lot of time and money without getting your message to those you want to hear and respond.

- Remember the aims you have chosen for your club (page 8). Target your publicity to help you begin to meet those aims.
- Make your publicity colourful and eye-catching: use the **POLar EXPLOrers** logo (available on the DVD or on the **POLar EXPLOrers'** website), an attractive font, pictures and clip art.
- The publicity team can also organise themed administration paperwork for the club: see *Holiday club admin* on page 19.

Publicity: in summary

Type of publicity	When	Useful for *your* club?
Posters/fliers	Before	
Direct letters or invitation cards, application forms, follow-up letters	Before	
School assemblies	Before	
Press releases	Before, during, after	
Church services and notices	Before	
Special church services	Before, after	
Social media	Before, during, after	
Prayer cards or alerts	Before, during, after	

External publicity: in detail

Posters/fliers

Use these to publicise **Polar Explorers** in your local area. Good for raising awareness generally, but not so effective at reaching your target audience.

Direct letters or invitation cards

Send or take a letter or invitation card to every child or family your church has contact with. Or distribute letters to all the children in your area, maybe through the local schools. (Make sure you do this well before the end of term, if you are having the club during school holidays.) The benefit of direct communication is that you will know this has reached your audience. If you enclose an application/registration form to be returned to you, your admin will be easier on the first day of your club.

You could also have a follow-up letter with more information, a consent/medical form and perhaps a **Polar Explorers** badge.

School assemblies

You may have a local Christian schools worker, or people from your church who are involved in schools ministry, or there may be church members who are teachers in the locality. If so, they could promote **Polar Explorers** in a school assembly, if the school is happy for them to do so.

- Do be clear about the capacity of your club, if numbers need to be restricted.
- Make sure your team are prepared to meet children who may not be used to a faith environment.
- If possible, involve the person who ran the assembly on the holiday club team so non-church children will have someone they recognise.

There are ideas for an assembly at the **Polar Explorers** website.

Press releases

Holiday clubs provide the kind of story that local radio and papers love to cover in holiday periods when news is scanty. This can increase the appeal of your holiday club and show that the church(es) involved are reaching out into your local community. A press story may run during or after your holiday club so may not help to bring children to the club.

Paid-for press advertisements are expensive, but may be worth considering if you are working with other churches, across your locality.

There's a sample press release at the **Polar Explorers** website.

Church services and notices

It's easy to forget to tell the people you know! Publicise the holiday club at your own church and other churches in your local area.

Special church services

On the Sunday before the first service of the club, include a section of the regular church service where the team will be formally commissioned. Recognition by the whole church family will give a practical and spiritual boost to the team.

Social media

Make use of any social media routes used by members of your church.

Consider setting up an invitation-only group or email list for your team, to circulate news, information and encouragement. For many people, this is a primary communication tool so make good use of it for your club.

Be aware of your church safeguarding policy and data protection issues (page 29).

Prayer cards or alerts

It is important to keep your church informed about the club. Prayer cards, bookmarks or emails can help church members pray before, during and after **Polar Explorers**. Again, be aware of your church safeguarding policy and data protection issues (page 29).

Publicity material

Turn to the inside back cover to find publicity materials available from Christian Publicity Organisation.

Visit the **Polar Explorers** website for logos and posters to print yourself.

Please mention Scripture Union in your promotional activity since positive publicity ultimately allows SU to develop more resources like this holiday club material.

Holiday club admin

These should use the same typeface and colours as other materials to maintain the consistent **Polar Explorers** scheme.

- Remember to budget for paper, printing and photocopying costs (it can mount up quickly).
- Get as much of this as possible done well before the club: printers have a nasty habit of going wrong at the last minute!

Before **POLAR EXPLORERS**

Item	Purpose	Quantity
Volunteer forms	For potential team members, including an indication of roles they'd like to take on	
Safeguarding forms	For team members who do not already have clearance	
Notes and training materials for the team	Even if someone else writes this material, the printing and publicity team should be responsible for the layout	

During **POLAR EXPLORERS**

Item	Purpose	Quantity
Registration forms	For children to complete	
Consent forms	For parents/carers/Huskies	
Collection slips	For parents/carers/Huskies	
Name badges	For the team members and for any adults who are on site and part of **POLAR EXPLORERS**	
Signs and notices	These will be needed around the site, including the main meeting area, entrances, toilets, exits and areas that are out of bounds	

Visit the **POLAR EXPLORERS** website to print registration forms, consent forms and collection slips.

Finances

Consider your financial resources. Work out what you need money for. Do you have a budget from your church? Will you need to do some fundraising? Will you charge for children to attend **POLAR EXPLORERS**?

Think about

The first child in a family could be charged, with a reduction for subsequent children.

Research shows that, in many cases, making a charge for a club has no effect on the number of children who come.

Parents often value a club they have had to pay for more highly than something that is free.

Item	Budget
Hire of premises	
Hire of equipment	
POLAR EXPLORERS resource books and DVD	
EXPEDITION LOGS and **TRAVEL LOGS**	
Publicity	
Craft materials	
Refreshments	
Scenery	
Printing and photocopying	
Prizes or presents for the children	

Legal requirements

There are various legal requirements you will need to be familiar with and conform to as you prepare for your holiday club. These include having a safeguarding or child protection policy in place, providing adequate space in your venue, meeting adult to child ratios, registering your club and insurance. To obtain up-to-date information on all of these requirements, go to 'Legal requirements for running a club' on the **Polar Explorers** website.

Remind all your team about these legal requirements – even those who are familiar with the venue and with working with children. Include it in your planning, briefings and any training you run.

Safeguarding

All churches should already have a clear safeguarding and child protection policy. Ensure that your holiday club team are familiar with it and it is carried out. Most churches have a designated safeguarding officer. Your holiday club team members need to know they should talk to this person first if they have any concerns about the safety or welfare of a child. For more information, go to the **Polar Explorers** website or the Churches' Child Protection Advisory Service www.ccpas.co.uk.

Talk with your church's safeguarding officer to make sure members of your team have the necessary paperwork, in good time for the club.

Data protection

How will you maintain the confidentiality of the information you receive on the registration forms? Make sure you abide by the principles of the Data Protection Act. Visit dataprotectionact.org for more information, including the eight principles of protecting data.

Accidents and first aid

Aim for there to be at least one person appointed as a first-aider (see page 18) with a current first aid certificate and access to an up-to-date first aid kit. (This is not a legal requirement but it is important to take reasonable precautions to oversee the welfare of those in your care.) The whole team should know who is responsible for first aid. You will need an accident book to record any incidents, which is essential in the event of an insurance claim. Each matter should be recorded, however small, along with details of the action taken. For other health and safety information visit www.rospa.com.

Risk assessment and fire procedures

The health and safety person on your team needs to make sure all the activities are adequately risk-assessed before the club starts and plan how you will evacuate the building in the event of a fire or other emergency. This person is in charge of clearing the building and dealing with the emergency services, but they should allocate responsibility for checking other areas of the building (toilets, snack bar and so on) to other team members who will be present each day.

Invent catchy slogans to remind the children where the toilets are, and what to do if the fire alarm sounds. One holiday club teaches: 'If there is a fire don't scream and shout, go through those doors and you'll soon get out.'

It is essential that the whole team knows emergency procedures, including fire exits and assembly points, and where to access a telephone in case of emergency.

- You may want to incorporate a fire drill into your programme early in the week. (The children will be used to this from school, but it might help the adults!)
- Check that fire escapes are kept clear.
- Make sure that the team know the position of fire extinguishers and know what the fire alarm – or noise that means 'leave the building immediately' – sounds like.
- Each Husky should be a roll-call marshal for their team.

Food hygiene

Refer to your church's health and safety policy if you are going to be cooking or handling food during the club.

BASICS 6
TIMETABLE/ PLANNER

Here is a sample timetable/planner for organising your holiday club.

This is an ideal, so don't feel put off if you haven't been able to start your planning as early as suggested. Work out how much time you actually have, then distribute the tasks below within it. This should give you a very

clear idea of whether or not you have sufficient time to plan *your* club.

And remember that the overall club coordinator will have a lot of checking to do – but it does not all have to be done by you!

POLAR EXPLORERS holiday club timetable/planner part 1

Date	Action	Notes
One year ahead	If you have just finished a club, make sure you have contact details for team and children; let them know you expect to hold a holiday club again.	
8 months before	'Pencil in' names for your core planning team.	
	Agree dates. Make provisional venue booking.	
	Confirm 'holiday club services' dates with church leader.	
	Request budget or launch fundraising.	
6 months before	Book assembly slot at local school(s).	
5 months before	Confirm members of core team; book first planning session.	
	Go into 'active organising' mode at church; launch prayer support.	
4 months before	**First core team meeting** (Decide theme; review or choose resources)	
	Order print and DVD resources.	
	Download further resources from website.	
	Hand out resource books to core team to read, reflect and pray.	
	Confirm venue booking.	
	Appoint publicity and printing person/team.	
	Liaise with church safeguarding officer to verify team paperwork.	
	Book anyone with specialist skills.	

POLaR EXPLOReRs holiday club timetable/planner part 2

Date	Action	Notes
3 months before	**Second core team meeting.** (Agree daily timetable; watch DVD and listen to theme song; confirm team roles.)	
	Appoint upfront presenters; technical manager; drama leader	
	Book 'whole team' planning meeting; invite all.	
	Check what equipment and resources are available.	
	Work out your 'shopping list' of specific items: see what people will donate before buying.	
10 weeks before	Have registration paperwork printed; or set up online registration.	
9 weeks before	Arrange provision for very young children of team members.	
8 weeks before	**Third core team meeting** (Further daily planning; plan extra events; consider contingencies [rainy weather etc]).	
	Confirm team members with specific roles and duties, ahead of 'all team' planning meeting.	
7 weeks before	Record and confirm applications and consent forms as they come in.	
6 weeks before	Assembly with local school(s), with application forms.	
	Brief the worship leaders for holiday club services.	
	Make sure any unusual items or equipment are arranged.	
5 weeks before	Final preparation for all-team meeting; prepare paperwork; plan agenda.	
	Start allocating children to groups.	
4 weeks before	**All-team meeting** (Run through everything; team training on **POLaR EXPLOReRs**; give theme song to band; agree set-up day; pray together.)	
	Communicate team lists and roles to all team; make sure all team have their briefing information.	
	Prepare checklist for 'set up' and 'clear away'.	
3 weeks before	Keep in touch with key team members and help problem solve.	
	Confirm details with service leader.	
2 weeks before	Monitor progress in all areas.	
Sunday before	Commissioning for all team during regular church service.	
1 week before	Final shopping.	
	Check signs, notes and lists are ready.	

POLar EXPLOrers holiday club timetable/planner part 3

Date	Action	Notes
Day before	Set up the venue as much as possible.	
1st service	Contribute to the service.	
Days of the club	Arrive early!	
	Attend team meeting before the club; give the day's briefing to all.	
	Monitor registration/children arriving.	
	Be available during the club session as the 'go to' person for any problems arising.	
	Keep track of time.	
	Monitor children leaving.	
	Help clear-up.	
	Short debrief on any key matters arising.	
	Thank and enthuse the team for the next session.	
	Make sure all is safe, clean and locked up for the next club session.	
Bonus event(s)	(eg) Games, fun, barbeque for club families-and-friends, end of club party.	
2nd service	Contribute to the service.	
Afterwards	Help with final clear-up of the venue.	
	Sort out outstanding admin; balance budget.	
	Check follow-up press release has gone out.	
	Thank all the team personally.	
	Make sure you have contact details for team and children so you can invite them to other events, club reunions, special services and your next holiday club.	
	Informal review meeting for full team, perhaps with a meal, to evaluate the club.	
	… and relax!	

Thanks to all the holiday club coordinators who helped compile this timetable, especially Jenny, Simon, Shera and Margaret.

EXPEDITIONS

SERVICE 1
Never too Hopeless
TO BE PART OF GOD'S BIG EXPEDITION

Explorers' **background**

For children with no church background

Children and adults will have come to church for a number of different reasons. Adults may have come to bring their child but have no interest themselves in faith matters. Alternatively, they might be exploring the idea of faith in God, and registering their child for **POLar EXPLOrers** may be part of that journey. Both children and adults will have mixed ideas and experiences of what church looks and feels like and what Christianity is all about. Each person needs to be welcomed and helped to feel a part of the service. Bear in mind that lots of what is familiar to a regular church attendee will be completely alien to those who have never been before – and even to those who have been to other churches but not yours. Try and be as accessible as you possibly can.

For church children

Encourage church children to be on the lookout, not only for their friends who wouldn't usually come along, but also for other children and their families who they haven't yet met. Encourage your regular families to invite new families to come and sit with them. You may wish to ask some of the church children and families to take part in the service to help them feel a shared ownership of the holiday club.

For children with other faiths

Muslim children *may* have been told that Judas rather than Jesus died on the cross or that Jesus had just passed out and recovered in the tomb. Reiterate that professional Roman soldiers would not have been wrong about him being dead. Emphasise that the soldiers speared Jesus in the side. He really was dead and really did rise.

Hindu and Tibetan Buddhist children *may* believe that Jesus' soul migrated to another body – although reincarnation usually involves being reborn as a baby (Hinduism) or the soul coming into an infant or small child (TB). Ensure they know this was Jesus in the same body, but initially, perhaps because they did not expect to see him, Jesus' followers did not recognise him.

Jewish children *might* ask what Jesus explained from their Scriptures (see: Genesis 3:15; Genesis 22:9; Jesus is the substitute sacrifice: Isaiah 53; Daniel 7:12–14).

For children with additional needs

Identify a champion who sees children with additional needs, not as a difficulty to be dealt with, but a privilege to be part of. The 'Never too' theme of **POLar EXPLOrers** will resonate with children who need extra assistance. Those who seem weaker are indispensible to God's big expedition. The additional needs champion should welcome children with specific needs or who appear overly anxious about entering church. Their families will also be anxious and are best able to say what is needed for successful inclusion. Identify a 'safe' part of church where it is not too noisy or crowded – a place where children can go for a 'timeout' when they need to get away.

SERVICE 1 **preparation**

Key passages
Luke 24:13–34; Matthew 28:18–20

Key storylines
- Jesus has been crucified and resurrected.
- He appears to his followers – specifically in the episode on the road to Emmaus.
- Jesus commissions his followers to be disciples who make disciples.

Key aims
- To outline the events of Jesus' death and resurrection, and his great commission to his followers.
- To launch the holiday club so that church members know how to pray for it in the coming week(s).
- To welcome any children and their associated adults coming to the club who are not usually part of the worshipping community.

WHAT-YOU-NEED CHECKLIST:
- ☐ A large cross or the facility to project one
- ☐ Four Bibles and readers
- ☐ A large candle, matches, tea lights
- ☐ Cards with these words on: Suffering, Endurance, Character, Hope, Holy Spirit, Love; and these symbols: an arrow, an equals sign, a plus sign (you can download these from the **POLar EXPLOrers** website)

SUGGESTED SONGS
Songs should be ones that give a strong gospel message. Be aware that visitors may not know songs and may not want to sing words that they don't understand or believe. Ideally, try to have a mix between the old and the new.
- 'God made you and me', *Light for Everyone* CD
- 'So amazing God', *Light for Everyone* CD
- 'Who was the man?', *Light for Everyone* CD
- 'Anyone can come to God', *Reach Up!* CD
- 'God's love is big', *Great Big God 3* CD
- 'There is a Redeemer', *Songs of Fellowship* 544
- 'Thine be the glory', *Songs of Fellowship* 551
- 'Searching for your truth', the **POLar EXPLOrers** theme song

SERVICE 1

SERVICE 1 **programme**

Welcome

Welcome everyone to the launch of **POLar EXPLOrers**. Talk a little about the holiday club so that everyone is aware of what's happening and when. The theme of the club will be introduced in this service. Start with a song that recognises that God welcomes everyone to come and worship as part of his family.

You may also like to introduce the drama *The Ice Adventure* that will be running throughout the club, and invite the drama team to perform the short sketch available for today (see script on pages 77 and 78).

Set the scene

Have a large cross (or project a picture of a large cross) somewhere obvious. Ask if anyone can tell you why the cross is the symbol of the Christian faith. Can anyone give a really concise explanation of the good news of the Christian faith?

Depending on how well they do, you might want to pull out the points that:

- God created us (humanity) to be in a relationship with him.
- We decided we'd prefer to do our own thing than follow God's ways, which were designed to keep us safe.
- And so, we became separated from God.
- God sent Jesus to identify with us fully as a man, so that he could pay the price for all the things we had done that had separated us from God.
- Jesus was crucified on the cross.
- Three days later Jesus rose from the dead to prove that we are no longer separated from God if we trust in him, and we will live with him for ever and ever.
- This is the good news!

Bible reading

Create a dramatised reading of Luke 24:13–35, using the Contemporary English Version or another child-friendly translation. You will need four people: a narrator, Jesus, Cleopas and the other disciple. It is very obvious where each character reads in the text.

Talk

At the beginning of the talk, bring a large, lit candle to a central position. Speak from very close to it.

These disciples were devastated: they had followed Jesus, believing he was someone very special sent to rescue God's people, but they felt as if all their hopes had been dashed. Jesus was dead and none of the things he'd promised had happened. They must have wondered what on earth they were going to do next. So they felt utterly hopeless.

Blow out the candle.

And then there's another guy walking beside them: he seems to be completely clueless about what has just happened. Yet as they talk together, something begins to stir inside of them.

Take out a box of matches and be trying to strike one as you speak, but make sure it doesn't light until you get to the crucial point!

The Bible says that they felt their hearts were warmed – hope started to stir in them. As they hear the man explaining God's Word to them, they begin to experience the sensation that perhaps all is not lost. Perhaps there is a way forward! And then that tiny ember explodes into flame. The man breaks bread at the start of a meal and suddenly the disciples realise who it is – Jesus!

Finally, light the match and relight the candle.

Paul, one of Jesus' followers a little bit further on in the story, has something to say about hope:

'We gladly suffer, because we know that suffering helps us to endure. And endurance builds character, which gives us a hope that will never disappoint us. All of this happens because God has given us the Holy Spirit, who fills our hearts with his love' Romans 5:3–5.

At this point in the talk, you will need your word and symbol cards.

We all know that there are times in life when we suffer, and these two disciples were in that time right then.

Ask for a volunteer to come and hold the Suffering card.

They were suffering one of life's lows, they were having to endure what felt very painful indeed.

Give the first volunteer an arrow card for their other (left) hand and ask a second volunteer to come and hold the Endurance card to the left of the first person.

Their characters were not enjoying the stretch on them that was taking place.

Give your second volunteer an arrow for their left hand and ask a third volunteer to come and hold the Character card to the left of the second person.

But into that suffering and endurance and opportunity for character growth comes Jesus who gives them their hope back.

Ask the person who played Jesus in the Bible reading to come and hold the = and the Hope cards.

A friend of Jesus is never really alone. Jesus has beaten death and anyone who asks him to forgive them can have a new, fresh start.

But this Paul doesn't stop there. He tells us what happens next in the story: God gives the Holy Spirit and his people's hearts are filled with love – not just love for God but love for the world around them and a desire for that world to know God's love, too.

Ask for a couple of final volunteers to come and hold the Holy Spirit, + and Love cards.

Invite your narrator back and ask them to read Matthew 28:18–20.

The disciples took this really seriously! During the club we're going to be finding out about God's big expedition: how Jesus' friends went out to help people of many, many nations to start being friends of Jesus too. We're going to be looking at some of the expeditions they went on and see how what they did has made a massive difference to millions of people's lives throughout the years. And Jesus' friends are still part of God's big expedition!

We're going to be using a phrase this week that tells us that, no matter what people say, we are never too *anything* to be Jesus' friend and part of God's big expedition. Today, let's remember that we are never too hopeless to be part of God's big expedition.

Response

Give people a few minutes to reflect on the things that they feel hopeless about. Have a basket of tea lights beside your candle and invite them to come and light a tea light from your candle. Depending where they are on their faith journey, they could simply be saying that they will think a bit more about this Jesus or they could be inviting Jesus to help them feel his hope within them, either again or for the first time. Make sure it is easy for people to opt out of this activity if it is not something they are comfortable with.

If it works in your context, it would be ideal to have people on hand to pray with anyone who feels like they would like to invite Jesus to be their friend for the very first time.

Prayer

Pray for everyone who's going to be a part of your **Polar Explorers** club, that they would let Jesus give them hope and they would know that he invites them to be his friend and part of his big expedition.

Ask anyone involved in running the club to stand up. Pray for them, that God would give them endurance, character and hope as they take part in the club.

EXPEDITION 1
Never too many mistakes
TO BE PART OF GOD'S BIG EXPEDITION

EXPEDITION 1 should be included for *all* **clubs.**

If you are going to miss out Expedition 3, you could include the gospel in today's Expedition (and/ or during Expedition 2). For today, place the gospel message in *Key data*, **leaving space at the end of the programme for children to respond. You could say:**

'Peter made lots of mistakes, but Jesus forgave him and Peter went on to tell thousands of people about Jesus: God wants to be our friend, but we are always messing things up. These things that we do wrong – the Bible calls them 'sin' – stop us being friends with God. So Jesus came to earth. He did nothing wrong, but he took the punishment in our place. He was killed on a cross but God brought him back to life. Because of what Jesus did, we can be forgiven for all the things we have done wrong, and be friends with God.'

Explorers' **background**

No church background

Children from outside a church community may have a picture of Christians being people who try to do things right and tell people off who they think are getting things wrong. Peter's story illustrates that people who really mess things up can still be friends with God. Some children may feel that they are not able to live up to the requirements of being a follower of Jesus, but this story should challenge them.

Church children

Some church children may have the opinion that they would never deny Jesus like Peter did; others may struggle with the feeling that they are not as good a Christian as the others around them. What's so vital to stress is that nothing we do can prevent God from loving us. Some older children may be starting to feel that church is boring and not for them; we need to help them to understand just how exciting it is to be part of God's big expedition.

Other faiths

Jewish children may pick up on quotes from their Scriptures. Point out that Jesus and his closest followers were Jews, whose experiences gave them insight into Scripture. The quotes demonstrated how they saw God at work in and through Jesus and the Spirit.

Arab and Asian children may ask why Asians and Arabians were in the crowd – tell them that God loves the whole earth, every tribe, tongue and nation, and wants all people to come to him, not just one group. Christianity is not European.

In Judaism, one can only forgive sins against oneself. In Islam, forgiveness is encouraged, but proportional revenge can be taken. Buddhists and Hindus practise forgiveness for the sake of their spiritual life and in Jainism, forgiveness is a core value.

The Trinity is complicated for everyone – see *Top Tips on Explaining the Trinity* for ideas, in case anyone asks!

Additional needs

Brief small group leaders and identified one-to-one helpers, explaining confidentially the specific needs of the child and strategies that will support inclusion. Create a safe space in your venue – denote it with a small carpet (IKEA circle carpets are ideal), beanbags etc. Provide a resource pack which includes picture symbols showing event activities, small plastic figures to act as 'fiddle friends' and ear defenders for use by a hypersensitive child. Give plenty of warning before changes of activity. Sudden change can provoke anxiety, resulting in 'fight or flight' behaviours. Use the safe space for a child that needs five minutes time out to feel OK again, especially as today we are learning about messing up and being restored.

EXPEDITION 1 **preparation**

Key character and passages
Peter – Matthew 16:18; John 18:1–27; Acts 2

Key storylines
- Peter was one of Jesus' closest friends and followers but he made an awful lot of mistakes. When Jesus had been arrested, before he was crucified, Peter denied that he even knew Jesus.
- When the Holy Spirit came, Peter preached an amazing message to all the people, many came to know Jesus and the early church was formed.
- We need to have the right equipment/clothing for the expedition we are going on.

Key aims
- To welcome the children and set the tone for the club.
- To help the children understand that, however much we have messed up in the past, God can restore us and use us in ways we never dreamed of.
- To help the children begin to explore that we are never too *anything* for God to use us.
- To help the children begin to understand the concept of a Kingdom Footprint: how what we do with God leaves positive marks on the world around us.

. . . .

Husky time
Spiritual preparation
Read John 18:25–27 and John 21:7,15–17.

Talk about how Peter must have felt when he realised he'd denied Jesus – just as he had sworn he wouldn't. Ask the leaders these questions:
- What emotions might Peter have experienced in meeting Jesus after the resurrection?
- Is Jesus' reinstatement of him surprising or not?

- How do you think Peter got from denying Jesus to standing up, preaching and leading thousands of people to know Jesus in Acts 2?
- Where are you in this story? Are you with Peter denying Jesus? With Peter in front of the crowds on Pentecost? Or somewhere in between?

Say that there are times when we have all failed to do what we know God wants us to do, and felt that we would never be useful for anything again – and certainly not good enough to serve God. There may be people in your team who are feeling like this. Spend a moment in quiet to help people reflect on Peter's transformation and what that might mean for us.

Children aren't exempt from these experiences and feelings, and there may well be children coming today who feel (even at their young age) that they are good for nothing. Spend a few minutes allowing each person to listen for God's words of affirmation and love over them. Then pray for the children coming today – that they would know that they can never make too many mistakes to be accepted by God.

Practical preparation
Talk through the programme, making sure that everyone understands the activities and has the resources to deliver them if necessary. Check that younger team members don't feel too daunted by what's ahead and that they know where they can go to ask for help. Make sure everyone knows they can ask questions!

Set up all the different areas in the club, making sure you are ready for when the first children arrive. As this is the first morning, you will need to have your registration procedures well understood by all of the team so that children and parents feel secure as you welcome them. If you have arranged extra helpers for today, make sure they are clear about what they are doing.

WHAT-YOU-NEED CHECKLIST

- [ ] **Registration**: registration forms, badges, labels, pens, expedition team lists, extra helpers
- [ ] **Expedition team leaders**: big sheet of card or paper, marker pens (for team name), Bibles, **Travel Logs** or **Expedition Logs**, a book of baby names (for 8 to 11s groups), a big rucksack and scarf and gloves (for 5 to 8s groups), a large blank footprint
- [ ] **Basic training**: two full sets of clothes
- [ ] **Data report**: a whiteboard for ongoing list of things needed for an expedition, a digital camera and the means to print photos during session
- [ ] **Technology**: PA system, projection system for PowerPoints, song words etc, **Polar Explorers** DVD
- [ ] **Music**: Poles Apart band or backing tracks
- [ ] **Drama**: costumes and props
- [ ] **Activities**: equipment for games and construction
- [ ] **Sir Random and Bare Feet**: running order, *Learn and remember* verse, a box of shoes (including a pair of running shoes)
- [ ] **Adventure tales**: DVD (or the story script and headlines stuck onto three newspapers, three leaders)
- [ ] **Key data**: whiteboard for ongoing list of key data
- [ ] **Radio transmission**: a bin
- [ ] **Uploaded data stream box**: for jokes, messages, footprint pictures
- [ ] **Refuelling station**: drinks and snacks
- [ ] **Photographer**: digital camera

EXPEDITION 1 **programme**

Do you copy?
10 minutes

As this is the first day, it will be ideal if you can have extra helpers to register children and introduce them to their Husky (expedition team leader). It is important that the small-group leaders are available for their group members and not engaged in registration activities.

Each expedition team will have their own area, [team name] HQ, which they can decorate as they choose. Ideas for decoration can be found on page 13.

In this first group time, the groups should come up with a team name together. Provide a large sheet of card or heavy paper and art materials for the children to make a poster displaying the team name. Put the poster up in the team HQ. The group might also like to come up with explorer nicknames for themselves – or you could do this as the week progresses.

. . . .

Base camp
45 minutes all together

Situation report
Once all the children are settled, Sir Random Finds and Bare Feet introduce themselves and welcome the children to the club.

Share any club rules or important information. It may be worth having three key rules, such as:
- What to do in the event of the fire alarm sounding
- Toilets – where are they and whether you need to ask before you go
- No interrupting others if they are talking in a discussion setting.

Sir Random Finds tells the children that they are **POLar EXPLorers** on an expedition team. During the club they are going to be finding out about God's big expedition: how Jesus' friends go out to help other people to start being friends of Jesus too.

Each day this week (*or however often you are running the club*) they are going on a mini-expedition together to find out about one of those friends and discover just how exciting it is to be a friend of Jesus and be part of God's big expedition.

Basic training
Have two sets of explorers' clothes in piles at the front. This might include thermals, salopettes, walking trousers, ski jackets, waterproof jackets, boots, gloves, hats, sunglasses, but make sure you have the same articles in each pile. Ask two Huskies to come up and race to put the clothes on. Use a stopwatch to record the winning time, and the time for the other Husky. Write the names and the times on strips of paper and stick them in the correct position on a leader board.

Data report
Sir Random Finds and Bare Feet introduce the children to their base camp set up, showing them their various boards of data and information. Bare Feet is trying to explain to Sir Random that she's here to study the carbon footprint – the way that what we do as humans affects the earth. Sir Random keeps getting mixed up with the terminology – things like cabin footprint, cardboard footprint, carbon blueprint etc.

Bare Feet is very excited about the whole idea and declares that she thinks she'll go out and get started right now – she heads for the door, but she isn't wearing any outdoor clothes and her feet are bare. Sir Random stops her and tells her she can't go out like that. He asks the children for ideas of what she should wear for her expedition. Sir Random explains that it's very important to have the right clothing and equipment before you embark on an expedition. He could share some mind-boggling statistics about the doom and destruction that faces you if you are unprepared!

Bare Feet dresses herself up in the clothes used in *Basic training*. Sir Random Finds starts a *Data checklist* for Bare Feet to remember what she

needs to help her on an expedition – he should write on it 'The right clothes and equipment'. He could also take a photo of Bare Feet dressed up and ready to go. This can be printed during the club and be put up for *Expedition debrief*. Bare Feet heads out into the wild.

Dancing on ice
Introduce the band, Poles Apart, and invite them to lead the children in the **POLar EXPLorers** theme song. Sing it a couple of times so that the explorers begin to get the hang of it, rather than singing other songs at this point.

Message from base
Sir Random tells one of his stories:

Did I ever tell you about the time when I was going to Siberia on a trip? Well it's extremely cold in Siberia and as I was the youngest member of the team, it was down to me to bring the thermal socks for everyone. I really thought I had packed them, but when we got there, I discovered that they weren't in my bag. What a disaster! Everyone was absolutely furious. They had to cut the sleeves off their extra jumpers to use for socks! I was only just starting out and I didn't think they would ever let me go on a trip again… What an enormous mistake to make. In fact, that reminds me of a story about someone in the Bible…

Adventure tales
Introduce the **POLar EXPLorers** DVD. In today's episode we meet Gemma and Blizz – the reluctant husky dog. Blizz is worried that he will never be good enough to be part of the sled team because he makes too many mistakes. Gemma tells him the story of Peter, and reassures him that he will always be given another chance.

If you have a talented storyteller on your team, you may wish also to tell the children the story. Either use the fully scripted retold Bible story for Expedition 1 on the **POLar EXPLorers** website or the storyteller could tell the story based on Matthew 16:18,

John 18:1–27 and Acts 2, using their own words if possible. They can use the section headings and interactive ideas from the script as memory joggers and to vary the story presentation each time.

If you are telling the story as well as using the DVD, tell the story first, then show the DVD so the children already have the outline of the events before seeing the episode.

Key data

Sir Random Finds then helps the children think about today's story using the key phrase 'Never too many mistakes to be part of God's big expedition'. He reminds the children that being part of God's big expedition is about being a friend of Jesus and going out to help other people to start being friends of Jesus too.

Peter was one of Jesus' best friends, but he messed up. When Jesus was in trouble, Peter said that he didn't know him, because he was scared. Peter must have thought it was the end – the end of his friendship, the end of Jesus, the end of what he believed in. But Jesus came back to life! And Jesus forgave Peter.

God used Peter to tell everyone about Jesus, and what he had done so that we could be friends with God. God has always wanted everyone to be good and loving and to do the right thing. But often we are not loving and do not do the right thing. Every one of us (except Jesus) has made mistakes that upset God – maybe been a cheat, told lies or been selfish, even though sometimes no one knows except us. Someone has to be punished for these wrong things.

Jesus took the punishment for all the things we have done wrong. If we are sorry for the wrong things we have done, we can never make too many mistakes that Jesus won't forgive us.

Add **'Never too many mistakes to be part of God's big expedition'** to your *Key data board* so that the children can remember it throughout the rest of the club.

Hear from the Husky

Bare Feet asks a leader to come up and share a story about how they made a mistake and pretended that they weren't a friend of Jesus, but God forgave them. The story could possibly include how they were able to go on and do something they didn't think they'd be able to because of the mistake.

Bare Feet can say she was glad that Sir Random stopped her from going out with no shoes on earlier – that would have been a big mistake to make! She can talk about the amazing footprints she made with her snowboots on. She can comment that when we go and do things for God we make special footprints on the world around us because we show other people what God is like. We are going to call these Kingdom Footprints. Lots of people's lives were changed because Peter left Kingdom Footprints – he did what God asked him to and told people about Jesus.

Learn and remember

The *Learn and remember* verse helps children to remember that God wants us to tell the world about Jesus and leave Kingdom Footprints.

Get out your box of shoes, which should include a pair of running shoes (the box needs to be shut with a hole cut in the top). Ask for a volunteer to come and pull one shoe out at a time until they find a running shoe. Keep reiterating the phrase 'shoes that are able to speed you on' – get the children involved in saying it as each shoe comes out – for example: 'Is this a shoe that is able to speed you on?'

Once both running shoes have been pulled out, display the whole verse on the screen and get everyone to read it out together.

'Wear shoes that are able to speed you on as you preach the good news of peace with God' Ephesians 6:15 (Living Bible).

There's also a song, 'Speedy shoes', on the **POLar EXPLORERS** website and DVD to help the children to learn the verse.

Expedition time
45 minutes

Refuelling station

Make sure the children are comfortable in their expedition teams as the Huskies help them with refreshments. Give children the opportunity to use the toilet. Younger children can take a long time over snack, so you may choose to begin your discussion as they are eating and drinking.

Bible exploration
With older children (8 to 11s)

Talk to the children about their names, and whether or not they know what their names mean. Have a baby names book on hand (or a smart phone and internet access) to find out any that the children don't know. There is space on page 8 in the **EXPEDITION LOG** for children to write down the meaning of their name.

Read Matthew 16:13–18 on page 9 of the **EXPEDITION LOGS**. Ask the children who the Son of Man is? (Jesus) Explain that everyone knew that there was someone really special coming, sent by God, called the Messiah. Jesus was that special person.

What does Peter's new name mean? Jesus wanted Peter to know what his job was going to be – he was going to be a leader of the church later on! What do you think he thought of that? Look back at what the children's names mean. Ask the children if they think their name meaning describes them, for example, Sophie means 'wisdom', so if you have a Sophie in your group ask her if she thinks she is wise.

Ask the children to remind you what Peter did wrong in today's story. (*He said he didn't know Jesus.*) How must Peter have felt when he realised what he'd done? Invite the children to draw two faces on page 10 – one of Peter when Jesus said he would be leader of the church and one when Peter said he didn't know Jesus.

Reiterate that Jesus forgave Peter and God used him to tell lots of people about what Jesus had done. Ask the children how they think Peter felt as he talked to the crowd.

If you have time, read the verses from Acts 2 on page 11 of the booklet. Encourage the children to do the puzzle on page 12.

With younger children (5 to 8s)

Read John 18:1–5,10–13,15–18,25–27. Invite the children to close their eyes and imagine the reading is a film playing in their imaginations. Ask the children how they think Peter felt when he had said three times that he didn't know Jesus.

On page 6 of the **Travel Log**, there are some sentences about the story. Some are right and some are wrong. Encourage the children to mark the sentences with a tick or a cross.

Ask the children to use the sentences to retell the story to each other. Think about the story you heard today. Did Jesus give Peter a special job to do after he went back to heaven? Yes he did. Peter was a leader of this group of people who followed Jesus. Now we would call those people the church. Peter spoke to lots of people and told them about Jesus, and lots of them believed in Jesus and became his friend because of what Peter said.

Read the story from Acts 2 on page 7. Then complete the dot-to-dot puzzle together on page 8, revealing what Peter did next. Describe what Peter said to the crowd, then ask the children to draw in lots of people listening to Peter. What kinds of expressions might these people have on their faces?

Ask the children if they can remember the first thing that's important for going on an expedition (the right clothes and equipment). Show the children the scarf and gloves you have, and put those in your expedition rucksack.

With all ages

- How do you think Peter felt after he said he didn't know Jesus?
- What about when Jesus came back to life?
- And when he stood in front of the crowd at Pentecost, telling them about Jesus?

- Have you ever done things that have made other people sad and upset?
- If you're already friends with Jesus, do you sometimes feel the wrong things you do, like telling lies and being selfish, stop you from following him?

Talk about what sort of difference Peter made to the world – his Kingdom Footprint. If we listen to Jesus, we can leave good marks on the world and other people and make a difference in Jesus' Kingdom. What sort of footprint did Peter leave? Come up with a phrase and write it on a large footprint shape. This can also be recorded on page 9 of the **Travel Log** and page 14 of the **Expedition Log**.

Radio transmission

Remind the group that Jesus still had an important job for Peter even though he made a big mistake. Ask the children to take a minute to think about some of the ways that they have messed up or made mistakes, maybe things that they know has upset someone else or something they know has upset God. Invite them to draw or write them down on a sheet of paper (explain that no one is going to see it). Say that God promises always to take these things away when we ask him to forgive us. We can still be a friend of Jesus and part of God's big expedition. Invite the children to destroy their sheets of paper – ripping or scrunching – and throw them in the bin.

Construction

Choose a construction activity from pages 70 to 73. There are two types of construction: **Polar Explorer** constructions that follow the theme of the club and can be done on any day, and Bible constructions that link with each Expedition's Bible teaching. Today's Bible construction is 'Flame headbands' on page 72. For more craft ideas, see *Ultimate Craft* (SU 978 1 84427 364 5).

Games

Help the explorers shape up by choosing suitable games from page 74 to 76. For more games ideas, see *Ultimate Games* (SU 978 1 84427 365 2).

Expedition debrief
25 minutes

Reporting back

In their exploration time, each team will have discovered what the Kingdom Footprint was for today's character. They will have written this on a large footprint. Sir Random Finds can invite a representative from each team up to share what their discovery of the Kingdom Footprint has been. He can transfer the information onto a footprint of his own and begin a trail of large footprints across the stage area. The children's footprints can be put up in their team HQs.

Uploaded data stream

The *Uploaded data stream* is the place for children to contribute their jokes, questions and comments to be used in this part of the programme. Today, you can introduce this and encourage the children also to add in their pictures of footprints of imaginary beasts – yetis, dinosaurs, that kind of thing. On this first morning, you might like to have a few contributions from leaders.

Dancing on ice

The band, Poles Apart, lead the children in a couple of lively songs.

Drama: *The Ice Adventure*

Introduce the comedy-drama, *The Ice Adventure*. If you didn't use the drama in the service, or if you feel that many of the children did not see the service episode, have that episode now.

In today's episode, the team discover that Helen Skelter has made lots of mistakes on previous expeditions. The Chief points out that everyone has their part to play in the expedition, no matter how many mistakes they've made in the past.

Radio scan

Explain that you are going to pray to God now. Say that we sometimes close our eyes when we pray so that we can concentrate and not get distracted by those around us. Say that even if a child doesn't want to concentrate on praying, it's nice to remain still and quiet to respect those that do. Explain that the children can say 'Amen' at the end if they agree with your prayer.

It would be good to pause and pray for people who feel that they have made too many mistakes to be involved with Jesus, who have done too many wrong and unloving things. Ask the children to close their eyes and imagine someone who has made mistakes. They can imagine them as a paper doll all scrunched up. Now ask them to imagine Jesus coming along and smoothing out the crumples. Say that this is like being forgiven by Jesus. Jesus will forgive anyone if they say they are sorry for the wrong things, and he'll be their friend.

Into the unknown
Ask the children to name as many different types of shoes as they can. Award points to the group that comes up with the most different types.

Alternatively, if you don't have too many children, get them to take off their shoes and put them into a big pile. The first person to find their shoes and put them on is the winner.

You might want to challenge the teams to see if they can already remember the *Learn and remember* verse!

Data upload
Remind the children of today's *Key data*: 'Never too many mistakes to be part of God's expedition'. Summarise the key points of the story and remind the children that, if we say we are sorry, Jesus will forgive the wrong things we have done. Ask the children to remind you what the first thing was that we need for an expedition.

Sir Random Finds reminds everyone about the collection procedure and says he is looking forward to seeing everyone next time when we'll go on another mini-expedition and find out about another of Jesus' friends. He then sends the children back to their teams HQs.

Over and out
10 minutes

Encourage the children to see who has the biggest feet. See if they can line themselves up with the biggest feet at one end and the smallest at the other.

Make sure that all the children have what they need to take home, including anything they made in the construction section. Ask the children what one thing they are going to share about **POLar EXPLOrers** when they get home. If you have time, the children can be starting to fill in the Explorer Fact File in their **Travel LOG** or **EXPeDITION LOG**.

Make sure you are available to talk to any children who want to respond to what they have heard today.

. . . .

Husky situation report
30 minutes

Once the children have gone, try to have a debrief as soon as possible: What went well? What didn't work quite as it should have? Are there any individual issues that the team need to be aware of? Ask the expedition leaders to share briefly how their team has settled in. Pray together and remember to encourage and affirm each team member in their role.

If possible, share a meal together, although this may only be possible on the final day. If your next session is the following day, make sure that any set-up or preparation is done before you release the team! Otherwise, remind everyone when and where you will next meet.

EXPEDITION 2
Never too ordinary
TO BE PART OF GOD'S BIG EXPEDITION

EXPEDITION 2 **should be included for** *all* **clubs.**

For a 3 or 4 day club: Adapt *Key data* **so that you include the gospel message from** EXPEDITION 3:

'And this is what Stephen told the people: God wants to be our friend, but we are always messing things up. Every one of us has been a cheat, told lies and been selfish, instead of being good and loving. These things that we do wrong – the Bible calls them 'sin' – stop us being friends with God. Someone has to be punished for these wrong things, so Jesus came to earth. He did nothing wrong, but he took the punishment in our place. He was killed on a cross – do you remember that from Peter's story? – but God brought him back to life. Because of what Jesus did, we can be forgiven for all the things we have done wrong, and be friends with God.'

And then carry on with Expedition 2.

Remember to give space later in the day's proceedings for children to respond, if they want to.

Explorers' **background**

No church background

Many unchurched children will be unfamiliar with the idea of 'roles' within a church other than a vicar-type person. The idea that members of the congregation, including the children, can do things for God may come as a surprise. Children can feel fairly insignificant, and this story may well be an encouraging one – that someone with such a background role had such an impact on the early church that he is written about in such glowing terms and remembered thousands of years later. He was no less on fire for God than the apostles who did all the 'up-front' ministry.

Church children

Children brought up in a church context may have some familiarity with this story, although they may be most familiar with the fact that Stephen was stoned. Children who are familiar with church may well aspire to an up front role, particularly in a contemporary setting where worship leaders can be seen as pop stars. They may think that these are the most spiritually significant people in the church and this story will encourage them to think about how each and every role has the potential for eternal significance.

Other faiths

All the main religions have groups of people who in English might be referred to as 'saints'. However, Christianity is in contrast with them all. Stephen is our exemplar, not just because of martyrdom or 'being full of the Spirit', but because he was drawn to practical service of others as well as devotion to God. In Buddhism, Hinduism, Sufi Islam, Jainism and Judaism, the people who might be called saints have either attained or seek to attain complete separation from the world or a degree of holiness that is almost godlike. Most adherents of other faiths will have no expectation of being like that.

In contrast, Christians are made righteous by God and he uses even imperfect people to share his message or serve his purpose.

Additional needs

Make a concentrated effort to learn the children's names and make a habit of using them to make each child feel special. Some children will have specific foods that they cannot eat. Children with cerebral palsy are prone to choking on certain foods. It would be good for the children to agree that they do not share their snacks so that there is no temptation for a child to accept something that is not safe for them.

Children with physical disabilities may feel that they are not able to contribute to the group. Every child has a key part to play offering friendship and encouragement to others. You may consider getting left-handed scissors or spring scissors to support children to do cutting out. If a child is physically unable to do the dressing-up race, place them in charge of the stopwatch.

EXPEDITION 2 **preparation**

Key character and passage
Stephen – Acts 6

Key storylines
- Stephen was chosen to help the apostles by organising the food.
- Although this didn't seem like a glamorous job, the Bible tells us that Stephen was full of the Holy Spirit, as well as grace and power, and did many signs and wonders.
- We need to have the right provisions for the expedition we are going on.

Key aims
- To welcome the children (back) to the club.
- To help the children understand that however unglamorous and in the background we feel, God will use us in amazing ways.
- To explore that God will give us his Holy Spirit to help us do whatever job he calls us to.
- To help the children discover Stephen's Kingdom Footprint.

. . . .

Husky time
Spiritual preparation
Ask the team to come up with a list of roles or jobs that people take on in a church setting. Invite them to rank the jobs in order of spiritual significance. Encourage people to be vocal in their defence of why they think what they do, but also to respect others' point of view.

Read Acts 6:1–7.

Ask everyone how they feel about the apostles' premise for getting other people to do this job. Encourage them to pull out the descriptions of Stephen from the passage (they can use descriptions in the rest of the chapter too, if they like). If someone came to them with that sort of reputation, which church ministry would they assign them to?

Ask the team members to think about their role on the **Polar Explorers** team. What kinds of qualities do they need to do this job well? In what ways could their roles be of eternal significance? Reiterate that, regardless of role, we are all working with God and equipped by him to fulfil our purpose. No one is more important than anyone else.

Ask the team to pray for each other in twos or threes, seeking God's blessing and encouragement for one another. Make sure those who prefer to pray silently feel able to do so.

Pray for the children coming today, that they would understand that, to God, every person is important and every job he asks them to do is important.

Practical preparation
Talk through the programme, making sure that everyone understands the activities and has the resources to deliver them. If you decided to make any changes from the previous session make sure everyone in the team knows about them. Check to see how younger team members got on and ensure that they have enough help and support. Make sure everyone knows they can ask questions!

In today's story about Stephen, both the DVD and the story script say that he was stoned but not specifically that he died. Decide in advance exactly what you are and are not going to say, and make sure that the team is briefed.

Set up whatever areas in the club need attention, making sure you are ready for when the first children arrive. Ensure that any activities from the previous expedition are well displayed both in the team HQs and at the front, as appropriate. You might like to have Sir Random Finds and Bare Feet wandering around in character speaking to the children as they arrive.

WHAT-YOU-NEED CHECKLIST
- [ ] **Registration**: registration forms, badges, labels, pens, expedition team lists
- [ ] **Expedition team leaders**: Bibles, **Travel Logs** or **Expedition Logs**, paper, marker pens, felt tips, scissors, rucksack and wrapped biscuits or other wrapped snacks for 5 to 8s groups, a large blank footprint
- [ ] **Basic training**: two full sets of clothes
- [ ] **Data report**: white board for ongoing list of things needed for an expedition, digital camera and the means to print photos during session
- [ ] **Technology**: PA system, projection system, song words etc, **Polar Explorers** DVD
- [ ] **Music**: Poles Apart band or backing tracks
- [ ] **Drama**: costumes and props
- [ ] **Activities**: equipment for games and construction
- [ ] **Sir Random and Bare Feet**: running order, porridge-making equipment, *Learn and remember* verse, box of snacks
- [ ] **Adventure tales**: **Polar Explorers** DVD (or the story script, five lunch boxes, headings on strips of paper, snacks)
- [ ] **Key data**: whiteboard for ongoing list of key data
- [ ] **Uploaded data stream box**: selected jokes, messages and footprint pictures
- [ ] **Refuelling station**: drinks and snacks
- [ ] **Photographer**: digital camera

EXPEDITION 2

③④⑤

45

EXPEDITION 2 **programme**

Do you copy?
10 minutes

Be ready to welcome your children back to their expedition team. Ask the children what they did after **Polar Explorers** last time and what they are looking forward to in today's session.

Use this time to continue to decorate your team HQ. Give each child (or pair) a large sheet of paper and invite them to draw expedition clothing and equipment. Encourage them to cut round their drawings and hang them up. As you work, chat about the club so far, then go on to discuss what sort of food and drink would be suitable for an expedition.

Base camp
45 minutes all together

Situation report
Sir Random Finds and Bare Feet re-introduce themselves to the children, reminding one another of what happened on the first expedition. They could talk about whether they slept well and ask the children if they did etc.

Sir Random Finds reminds the children about God's big expedition: how Jesus' friends go out to help other people to start being friends of Jesus too. On today's mini-expedition they will find out about a friend of Jesus called Stephen.

Basic training
Reveal your two sets of explorers' clothes in piles at the front. Look at the leader board from last time and comment on how good (or bad!) the Huskies were at completing their training. Invite two children up to race to get dressed in all the gear. Use a stopwatch to record the times and put today's contestants on the leader board.

Data report
Sir Random Finds looks at the *Data checklist* and reminds the children that it shows the things that will help Bare Feet on her expedition.

Sir Random and Bare Feet chat about their ongoing quest to gather information and data to learn more about this snowy wilderness, and how it may be affected by the idea of the carbon footprint. Even though Bare Feet tries to explain again to Sir Random about what it is she's here to study, he keeps getting mixed up.

Bare Feet says that she has been up all night thinking about her discoveries and she's really keen to get going today – she doesn't think she'll bother with breakfast. Today she is already wearing all the right clothes, including really ostentatious boots. Sir Random tells Bare Feet that breakfast is the most important meal of the day and that an explorer needs 6,000 calories a day: that's the same as 22 Mars bars!

Bare Feet takes the advice on board and makes herself some porridge. She should have a number of catastrophes and pantomime moments as she makes it! Sir Random Finds continues the *Data checklist* for Bare Feet to remember what she needs to help her on an expedition – he should write 'Food is Fuel'. He could also take a photo of Bare Feet with her porridge. This can be printed during the club and be put up during *Expedition debrief*. Finally, having eaten well, Bare Feet heads out into the wild.

Dancing on ice
The band, Poles Apart, lead the children in the **Polar Explorers** theme song. Depending on how much time you have, they could also include another song.

Message from base
Sir Random tells one of his stories:

Did I ever tell you about the time when I was going to Alaska on a trip? Well it's extremely cold in Alaska, and when you're very cold, you use half of your calories just to keep warm. As I was still quite a junior member of the team, it was up to me to make sure everyone had enough of the right things to eat. (*He asks the children to call out good explorer food suggestions: high-fat, high-calorie items are key, and things that are non-perishable.*) **I was a bit cross because it seemed like such a boring job but I know now that, without me, the trip would have been a disaster. You've got to have the right things to eat or you die in the cold! In fact, that reminds me of a story about someone in the Bible…**

Adventure tales
Introduce the **Polar Explorers** DVD. On the DVD today, Gemma and Blizz return from an exciting sled trip in the snow, but Blizz complains about the cold! Gemma tells him the story of Stephen to show that, when God is with us, we can do anything he asks of us. Even braving the cold!

If you have a talented storyteller on your team, you may wish to also tell the children the story. Either use the fully scripted retold Bible story for Expedition 2 on the **Polar Explorers** website or the storyteller could tell the story based on Acts 6 using their own words if possible. You can use the section headings and interactive ideas from the script as memory joggers and to vary your story presentation each time.

If you are telling the story as well as using the DVD, tell the story first, then show the DVD so the children already have the outline of the events before seeing the episode.

Key data

Sir Random Finds then helps the children think about today's story using the key phrase 'Never too ordinary to be part of God's big expedition':

Stephen's job seemed a bit ordinary – sharing out the food. Doesn't sound like he had a very glamorous job, does it? But the job was important and God was with Stephen. He gave Stephen the Holy Spirit so that he had all the help he needed to do the job and tell everyone about Jesus at the same time. Stephen did all that with words, and performing miracles too!

No matter what job God wants us to do, he will give us the Holy Spirit so that we have the help with which to do it.

Do you feel able or want to do what you need to? How about asking God to help you?

Sir Random reminds the children that Stephen's job seemed ordinary, and adds **'Never too ordinary to be part of God's big expedition'** to the *Key data board* so that the children can remember it throughout the rest of the club. He reminds the children about the *Key data* (never too many mistakes…) from the previous expedition.

Hear from the Husky

Bare Feet asks a leader to come up and share a story about a time when they were asked to do what seemed like an unimportant job but actually it was really important that they did it.

Bare Feet can say she was glad that Sir Random made her have breakfast before she went out earlier. It was extremely cold and she was glad to have that porridge inside her. She can comment that God gives us his Holy Spirit to help us to do things for him. Lots of people's lives were changed because the Holy Spirit helped Stephen do the job he was asked to do and feed people – even though it didn't seem like a very glamorous job.

Learn and remember

Have a box of snacks, some healthy and some not healthy. Ask the children to come and pull them out one by one,

and invite everyone to say whether this is healthy and good for an explorer or not healthy and bad for an explorer. Say that we need to be prepared well for the job God has asked us to do, just like an explorer needs to have the right food to be ready for adventure. God will give us his Holy Spirit to help us. Remind everyone that God's big expedition is to become a friend of Jesus and go out to help other people to start being friends of Jesus too.

Once all the snacks have been pulled out, display the verse on the screen and get everyone to read it out together.

'Wear shoes that are able to speed you on as you preach the Good News of peace with God' Ephesians 6:15 (Living Bible).

There's also a song, 'Speedy shoes', on the **POLAR EXPLORERS** website and DVD to help the children to learn the verse.

. . . .

Expedition time
45 minutes in small groups

Refuelling station

Make sure the children are comfortable in their expedition teams as the Huskies help them with refreshments. As you eat, chat together about what they have just experienced. The children may have some immediate questions that they'd like to ask. Make sure, though, that you give the children the chance to go to the toilet!

Bible exploration
With older children (8 to 11s)

Ask the children what they'd like to be when they grow up. Ask if anyone would like to be a dinner lady. It's unlikely that this will be their first choice! Ask why they wouldn't want to be a dinner lady or a waiter. Say that it isn't a very glamorous job – and you don't get paid very well. Ask if it is an important job. It actually is – because we all need to eat!

Ask the children to draw their favourite meal on the plate on page 15 of the **EXPEDITION LOG**. Challenge them to work out how many calories their meal

might be, using an app or website such as myfitnesspal.com (you will need to have preregistered with this website). You can then use the app/website to work out what kind of activity could be done on the calories in this meal, eg 20 minutes' running.

Read, or ask one of the children to read, Acts 6:1–8 on page 16. Encourage the children to underline anything that describes Stephen (don't forget the general things in verse 3). Talk about these things that describe Stephen. Are they important in dishing out food fairly? You wouldn't necessarily think so! But God's plan for Stephen was more than making sure everyone had what they needed. Ask the children what they think verse 8 means. See if they know about any miracles that Jesus did. It's quite possible that Stephen's miracles might have been similar. Who knows, maybe there were even food miracles like Jesus feeding the 5,000! Why could Stephen do the miracles? Was it really him?

The Bible says that Stephen was full of the Holy Spirit and that God gave him power. Remind the children that we heard about the Holy Spirit in the story in the previous session when the disciples had what looked like flames on them. Talk to the children about your experience of the Holy Spirit. Different churches will have differing views on the work, ministry and baptism of the Holy Spirit, so make sure that you are staying within the bounds of the church running the club. The key point here is that the Holy Spirit is our helper, sent to be with us when we decide to follow Jesus. He helps us to listen to and obey God and live the best life possible. He gives us all we need to do the jobs God gives us. We need the Holy Spirit to help us play our part in God's big expedition.

Talk about what kinds of things the Holy Spirit helps us to do. These might be quite ordinary things, though some people may do signs and wonders. Page 17 of the **EXPEDITION LOG** has space to write or draw these things.

Stephen told everyone about Jesus too. Ask the children if they've ever done this. If you have a group of children with little or no church background, take this opportunity to tell them about Jesus now. (You could say something like: God wants to be our friend, but we are always messing things up. Every one of us has been a cheat, told lies and been selfish, instead of being good and loving. These things that we do wrong – the Bible calls them 'sin' – stop us being friends with God. Someone has to be punished for these wrong things, so Jesus came to earth. He did nothing wrong, but he took the punishment in our place. He was killed on a cross – do you remember that from Peter's story? – but God brought him back to life. Because of what Jesus did, we can be forgiven for all the things we have done wrong, and be friends with God.)

Page 19 of the **EXPEDITION LOG** has a space for them to draw the 'Food for fuel' they need in their expedition rucksack. They can unscramble the words too.

With younger children (5 to 8s)

Talk to the children about what they like to eat. Encourage them to draw their favourite dinner on the plate on page 10 of the **Travel LOG**. Talk with the children about whether their food is healthy or unhealthy. Why is it important to eat healthy food?

Read Acts 6:2–7 to the group from page 11. Ask them what the problem was at the beginning of the story. How did the apostles fix it? Who did the disciples choose to help them? Follow the wiggly line to discover Stephen at the bottom of page 12.

What was special about Stephen? Why was he chosen? Did Stephen just do the food or did he do other very special things?

Say that Stephen was chosen because he was full of God's Holy Spirit. God sends the Holy Spirit to be with us when we decide to be a friend of Jesus – he's like a special friend, although we can't see him. The Holy Spirit helps all friends of Jesus to be like Jesus, so the Holy Spirit living in Stephen gave him all the help he needed to do the jobs that God asked him to do.

Ask the children what help Sir Random told Bare Feet she needed today. Show your biscuits or other snacks and put them in your expedition rucksack.

With all ages

- What's the biggest task you've been asked to do? How did you feel?
- Stephen told lots of people about Jesus. How would you have reacted if Stephen had told you about Jesus?

Talk with the children about what sort of difference Stephen made to the world. What sort of Kingdom Footprint did Stephen leave? Come up with a phrase and write it on a large footprint shape. There is also space in both the **Travel LOG** and **EXPEDITION LOG** to write or draw today's Kingdom Footprint.

Radio transmission

Remind the children that, if we are a friend of Jesus, the Holy Spirit lives with us and gives us all that we need to do what God asks us to. Say that the Holy Spirit can help us to decide to follow Jesus too. Give the children a few minutes quiet to listen and to say what they want to God. There is a space in both the **EXPEDITION LOG** (page 17) and **Travel LOG** (page 11) for children to write or draw anything that God says to them.

Construction

Choose a construction activity from pages 70 to 73. There are two types of construction: *Polar Explorer* constructions that follow the theme of the club and can be done on any day, and Bible constructions that link with each Expedition's Bible teaching. Today's Bible construction is 'Fruit pizzas' on page 72.

For more craft ideas, see *Ultimate Craft* (SU 978 1 84427 364 5).

Games

Help the explorers shape up by choosing suitable games from page 74 to 76. For more games ideas, see *Ultimate Games* (SU 978 1 84427 365 2).

Expedition debrief
25 minutes

Reporting back

In their exploration time, each team will have discovered what the Kingdom Footprint was for today's character. Sir Random invites a representative from each team to come and show their team's footprints and puts the information onto his own footprint.

Uploaded data stream

Choose a few jokes, pictures and messages from the data stream. Answer any questions that have been put into the stream. Encourage everyone to carry on uploading their contributions!

Dancing on ice

Invite Poles Apart to lead the children in a couple of lively songs.

Drama: *The Ice Adventure*

Introduce the next episode of *The Ice Adventure*. Today Great Scott secretly throws all the food over a cliff in an attempt to spoil the expedition. Prince Larry saves the day by having an extensive birthday feast in his bag.

Radio scan

God wants everyone to be part of his big expedition, to be a friend of Jesus and to tell others about Jesus. It would be good to pause and thank God that all the jobs on his expedition, whether they seem big or small, are important. Thank God that the Holy Spirit will help us be part of God's big expedition.

Explain that the children can say 'Amen' at the end if they agree with your prayer. Say that we sometimes close our eyes when we pray so that we can concentrate and not get distracted by those around us. Say that even if a child doesn't want to concentrate on praying, it's nice to remain still and quiet to respect those that do.

Into the unknown

Ask each expedition team to come up with the names of three good foods for an explorer. Ask them to jumble up the letters to create an anagram and write it in big letters on a sheet of paper so that it can be displayed at the

front. Gather the papers together and put them on a board at the front. See which team can unscramble the most words.

Data upload
Remind the children of today's *Key data*. Summarise the key points of the story and remind the children that the effect we have on the world when we do what God asks us is like leaving Kingdom Footprints. Ask the children to remind you what the second thing was that we need for an expedition (food that will help us). Say that God has given us the Holy Spirit to help us take part in his big expedition.

Sir Random Finds reminds everyone about the collection procedure and says he is looking forward to seeing everyone next tme when we'll go on another mini-expedition and see what sort of Kingdom Footprint another character from the Bible left on the world. He then sends the children back to their team HQs.

Over and out
10 minutes

Begin or continue (if you talked about this in *Bible exploration*) a conversation with the children about what they would like to be when they grow up. Is their chosen career important?

Make sure that all the children have what they need to take home, including anything they made in the construction section. Ask the children what one thing they are going to share about **Polar Explorers** when they get home. If you have time over, the children can be continuing to fill in their Explorer Fact File in their **Travel LOG**. Or you could carry on with any construction projects.

Make sure you are available to talk to any children who want to respond to what they have heard today.

Husky situation report
30 minutes

Once the children have gone, try to have a debrief as soon as is possible – What went well? What didn't work quite as it should have? Are there any individual issues that the team need to be aware of? Get the expedition leaders to share briefly how their team has settled in. Pray together and remember to encourage and affirm each team member in their role. Make sure that any set up or preparation for the next day, or the next club session, is done before you release the team!

EXPEDITION 3
Never too near or far
TO BE PART OF GOD'S BIG EXPEDITION

5 DAYS

For three or **four-day clubs, miss out** EXPEDITION 3.

Explorers' **background**

No church background

It is doubtful that children without any church background will know this story. It's an exciting one, however, especially at the end when Philip is miraculously transported to another city. As children, we often feel that many things are too far away and out of reach, but in this story we see that God used Philip to open doors far away by bringing him out of his usual context.

Church children

This isn't the most familiar story for church children and they may be surprised to discover it. Many children will be familiar with the concept of missionaries in other countries and they may or may not think that's an appealing idea. Regardless, other nations seem so far away and irrelevant to our lives here. This story shows us that by spending time with someone from far away, Philip opened a door for God's story to be told in another nation. The story shows us what can happen when we are ready to be used by God wherever he wants. Make sure the children understand that, although they are unlikely to be able to travel to exotic places, God can still use them.

Other faiths

It's unlikely children will ask about eunuchs, but in all the faiths other than Judaism, historically eunuchs were fully accepted as adherents. In Judaism, to worship, men had to be intact.

However, the fact that he had been to Jerusalem to worship shows perhaps those rules were occasionally bent.

Children of African heritage may be encouraged that this man took faith back to the heart of Africa and the Ethiopian church is one of the oldest in the world.

All of the major religions acknowledge prophets as people set aside by God or the gods to bring a message to humans. Christianity is rooted out of Judaism, so early believers carefully re-read Jewish Scripture to see where Christ was pointed to. Isaiah 53 and Psalm 22 seem to describe the suffering and death of the Messiah in ways not understood until the death of Jesus. This gives Philip the chance to speak of Jesus.

Additional needs

The children will now feel confident of the routine activities. Some may become overactive and benefit from redirection and possibly a five minute time out in the safe space to regain control. Keep a watching brief around the expedition teams for potential disruption. The word 'no' or 'stop' is often a 'wind-up' to hyperactive children and it is better to come alongside with a gentle smile and a positive instruction. For example, 'I would like you to sit' or 'I would like you to listen so that everyone can hear the story.'

EXPEDITION 3 **preparation**

Key character and passage
Philip – Acts 8:26–39

Key storylines
- **Philip had a very successful ministry preaching God's Word in Samaria, but God called him away to travel on a desert road.**
- **Because of Philip's obedience, the Ethiopian came to know Jesus.**
- **We need to have a compass to show us where we are on our expedition.**

Key aims
- **To welcome the children (back) to the club.**
- **To help the children understand that we can serve God wherever we are.**
- **To explore how Philip was ready to be used by God wherever he was.**
- **To help the children discover Philip's Kingdom Footprint.**

Husky time
Spiritual preparation
It would be ideal if you could get hold of a world map and gather your team around it. Talk about those that the team know who are serving God overseas. Invite them to point out where those people are. Ask the team if any of them have ever lived overseas (in an overtly missionary context or not) or if any of them feel that God might be asking them to work overseas.

Read Acts 8:1–13.

What does the passage tell us about Philip and his ministry? Encourage the team to think of similar figures in the Christian world today. Who might they be?

Read Acts 8:26.

How might Philip have felt to be called away from this successful ministry in Samaria? Would it have felt like a demotion? Has anyone ever been called out of a very public ministry? How did it feel?

Read Acts 8:27–40.

What was the significance of Philip's obedience? What happened?

Invite members of your team to share any testimony they have of God opening doors because of their willingness to obey and to go wherever he leads.

Ask the team to reflect on relationships they have with people who are curious about Jesus. What possibilities might arise from those relationships? Pray together for hearts to follow after God's leading and that doors will be opened to the good news of Jesus. Pray for children who don't yet know Jesus, that they might be curious to find out more about him. Pray for church children that are bringing their non-church friends to the club, that they would have good conversations and feel confident about explaining who Jesus is.

Practical preparation
Talk through the programme, making sure that everyone understands the activities and has the resources to deliver them if necessary. Check that younger team members don't feel too daunted by what's ahead and that they know where they can go to ask for help. Make sure everyone knows they can ask questions!

Commitment booklets, such as Scripture Union's *Friends with Jesus* and *Me + Jesus*, will be helpful in this session. If you are planning to use these, make sure the team members know what is available and which age group they are suitable for.

Set up all the different areas in the club, making sure you are ready for when the first children arrive. Ensure that any activities from previous expeditions are well displayed both in the team HQs and at the front, as appropriate. You might like to have Sir Random Finds and Bare Feet wandering around in character speaking to the children as they arrive.

WHAT-YOU-NEED CHECKLIST
- [ ] **Registration**: registration forms, badges, labels, pens, expedition team lists
- [ ] **Expedition team leaders**: Bibles, **Travel logs** or **expedition logs**, paper, marker pens, felt-tip pens, scissors, double-sided tape, local maps, compasses, rucksack, compass for 5 to 8s groups, small toy characters for 5 to 8s, paint and clean-up facilities (optional)
- [ ] **Basic training**: two full sets of clothes
- [ ] **Data report**: whiteboard for list of things needed for an expedition, digital camera and the means to print photos during session
- [ ] **Technology**: PA system, projection system for PowerPoints, song words etc, **Polar explorers** DVD
- [ ] **Music**: Poles Apart band or backing tracks
- [ ] **Drama**: costumes and props
- [ ] **Activities**: equipment for games and construction
- [ ] **Sir Random and Bare Feet**: running order, enormous compass made out of card, *Learn and remember* verse, box of toy vehicles, a world map of some kind
- [ ] **Adventure tales**: **Polar explorers** DVD (or the story script, locations of the story set up with brown cloth, blue cloth, some kind of vehicle or umbrellas)
- [ ] **Key data**: whiteboard for ongoing list of key data
- [ ] **Uploaded data stream box**: selected jokes, messages and footprint pictures
- [ ] **Refuelling station**: drinks and snacks
- [ ] **Photographer**: digital camera

EXPEDITION 3 **programme**

Do you copy?
10 minutes

Be ready to welcome your children back to their expedition team. Ask the children what they did after **POLar EXPLORERS** last time and what they are looking forward to in today's session.

You can use this time to continue to decorate your team area. Encourage the children to create footprints. Invite them to draw around their feet and colour them in. Alternatively, if you are feeling adventurous, help them to paint their feet and print them on paper. You could do this using trays of paint and sponges; careful thought will need to be given to cleaning and drying the children's feet in time for *Base camp*.

Cut round the footprints and tape them to the floor. Talk with the children about what direction various things are from where you are just now. Which way is the town centre, the park, their school etc?

- -

Base camp
45 minutes all together

Situation report
Sir Random Finds and Bare Feet re-introduce themselves to the children, setting the tone for the session, perhaps talking about discoveries made on previous days or even just more general things like what they had for breakfast!

Sir Random Finds reminds the children about God's big expedition: how Jesus' friends go out to help other people to start being friends of Jesus too. On today's mini-expedition they will find out about a friend of Jesus called Philip.

Basic training
Reveal your two sets of explorers' clothes in piles at the front. Look at the leader board and comment on how good (or bad!) everyone has been so far. Ask two Huskies to race to get dressed in all the gear. Use a stopwatch to record the times and put today's contestants on the leader board.

Data report
Sir Random Finds looks at the *Data checklist* and reminds the children that it shows the things that will help Bare Feet on her expedition.

Sir Random and Bare Feet continue to chat about the idea of the carbon footprint. Sir Random is still getting mixed up with this. Bare Feet is keen to get out again – today she has had her breakfast and has the right clothes on for her expedition. Sir Random asks her where she'll be going today. Bare Feet says she thinks she'll follow last time's footprints. Sir Random is horrified that Bare Feet would rely on something like that – footprints can disappear so easily in a fresh snowfall. Sir Random gets out a huge compass and asks Bare Feet if she knows what it is. There can be a pantomime moment here of her guessing incorrectly several times – the children will probably shout out the right answer too.

Sir Random explains that a compass helps you to know where you are. He shows Bare Feet that if you know the direction or bearing that you've taken on the way somewhere, you should be able to get back just fine by coming in the exact opposite direction on the way back.

Bare Feet takes the advice on board and has a bit of practice using the compass to direct her across the room and back – she could bang into things as she concentrates on the compass. Sir Random Finds continues the *Data checklist* for Bare Feet to remember what she needs to help her on an expedition – he should write on it 'Compass for location'. He could also take a photo of Bare Feet with her compass. This can be printed during the session and be put up for the *Expedition debrief* section. Bare Feet heads out into the wild.

Dancing on ice
The band, Poles Apart, lead the children in the **POLar EXPLORERS** theme song.

Message from base
Sir Random tells one of his stories:

Did I ever tell you about the time when I was going to the South Pole on a trip? Well, on that occasion, I never even got to go! The team leader called me and said that they wanted me to go somewhere else entirely and train somebody who would be going. I was a bit put out, as it happened – I really wanted to go on the trip – but I did as I was asked and trained up another chap to go on the trip. Smashing bloke, he was! In fact he was so smashing that the trip was hugely successful and they discovered all sorts of top stuff. I would have loved to have been there but do you know, I found out that I could make a difference wherever I was! In fact, that reminds me of a story about someone in the Bible…

Adventure tales
Introduce the **POLar EXPLORERS** DVD. Today, Gemma and Blizz are feeling tired after a long journey on the sled, but they have seen some amazing sights. Gemma tells Blizz the story of Philip, and explains that wherever we find ourselves, God wants to use us to do great things for him.

If you have a talented storyteller on your team, you may wish to also tell the children the story. Either use the fully scripted retold Bible story for Expedition 3 on the **POLar EXPLORERS** website or the storyteller could tell the story based on Acts 8:26–39 using their own words if possible. You can use the section headings and interactive ideas from the script as memory joggers and to vary your story presentation each time.

If you are telling the story as well as using the DVD, tell the story first, then show the DVD so the children already have the outline of the events before seeing the episode.

Key data

Sir Random Finds then helps the children think about today's story using the key phrase 'Never too near or far to be part of God's big expedition':

When Philip did what God asked him to, he met the Ethiopian official and changed his life! The official was reading something from the Bible which talked about Jesus, but he didn't understand what it was all about. God sent Philip to help him understand the good news. And this is what the good news is.

God wants to be our friend, but we are always messing things up. Every one of us has been a cheat, told lies and been selfish, instead of being good and loving. These things that we do wrong – the Bible calls them 'sin' – stop us being friends with God. Someone has to be punished for these wrong things, so Jesus came to earth. He did nothing wrong, but he took the punishment in our place. He was killed on a cross – do you remember that from Peter's story? – but God brought him back to life. Because of what Jesus did, we can be forgiven for all the things we have done wrong, and be friends with God. That's what Philip told the Ethiopian. Because Philip was willing to do what God wanted, the Ethiopian learned about Jesus and became friends with God!

Write the phrase, **'Never too near or far to be part of God's big expedition'** on your *Key data board*.

Hear from the Husky

Bare Feet asks a leader to come up and share a story about a time when they did what God asked and something amazing happened. If no one has a story like this, you could ask someone to give their testimony – who was it that told them the good news, like Philip did?

Bare Feet can say she was glad that Sir Random made her take the compass today – it helped her to travel in lots of different directions without getting lost! The compass reminds us that we can serve God wherever we find ourselves, just as Philip did.

Learn and remember

Have a box of toy vehicles, plus a doll (such as an action man) and some kind of animal-drawn vehicle. Have enough vehicles to stick one word from the *Learn and remember* verse to the bottom of each one. Ask one of the expedition teams to come out and put the vehicles in order of which travels the fastest. Remind the children that, in today's story, Philip was willing to do what God wanted, and he travelled to tell someone about Jesus. Turn the vehicles over and see if anyone can rearrange the words into the verse.

There's also a song, 'Speedy shoes', on the **POLar EXPLorers** website and DVD to help the children to learn the verse.

. . . .

Expedition time
45 minutes in small groups

Refuelling station

Make sure the children are comfortable in their Expedition Teams as the Huskies help them with refreshments. As you eat and drink, chat together about the club so far, and what they have enjoyed about **POLar EXPLorers** today. Give the children the chance to go to the toilet.

Bible exploration
With older children (8 to 11s)

Have a large map of the world. Talk to the group about where they would really like to go. Is there anywhere they really, really wouldn't want to go? They can mark up their own maps on page 21 of the **EXPeDITION LOG**.

The passage for today's story is on pages 22 to 24 of the booklet. It has spaces for the children to fill in emoticon faces for the characters at various points. You can find examples of emoticons on the **POLar EXPLorers** website.

Read the passage together, pausing for the children to draw their emoticons. When you have finished reading, invite the children to tell you why the Ethiopian needed Philip's help. Challenge them to remember the things Philip told the Ethiopian about Jesus. Ask the children what things they would have told the Ethiopian about Jesus. Discuss this together,

then encourage the children to write their ideas in the speech bubbles on page 25.

Say that yesterday (or whenever you did Expedition 2) we talked about the Holy Spirit giving us everything we need for our journey with God. Today, God sent the Holy Spirit to help Philip, and we can ask God for help, too. Talking to God is called praying. Praying isn't anything scary or fancy, it's just talking. You don't have to use any special words or a different voice. You can close your eyes if you want to, but you don't have to. You can do it anywhere!

On page 26 of the booklet, there are some thought bubbles for the children to fill in of things they might talk to God (pray) about in various situations. Invite the children to draw the compass in the rucksack on page 27 and unscramble the words.

If you have any children in your group who want to know more about the good news of Jesus, you could spend some time chatting about it. You might wish to have the booklets detailed on the inside front cover handy to help children think more about becoming friends with God.

With younger children (5 to 8s)

Talk to the children about places they've visited. Where did they really like? Is there anywhere they wouldn't want to go again? Invite them to write a postcard from a favourite place. If they are very young, they can just write 'Love from' and their name. They can draw a scene on the front of the postcard too. The template for this is on page 14 of the **TraveL LOG**.

Tell the children the story again from Acts 8:4–7,26–40 – either in your own words or from the Bible. Use some small toy characters to play it out.

The Ethiopian had lots of questions about Jesus. Philip helped the Ethiopian to understand about Jesus. Who do we ask for help when we don't understand something? On page 16, there are some pictures of people. Invite the children to colour in the people they would ask for help in understanding something.

Say that God can help us too. When we talk to God, it's called praying. You can pray anytime, anywhere and about anything. You don't have to put on a funny voice or use big words. You can just talk to him like anyone. Ask the children what sort of things they might talk to God about. At the bottom of page 16, there is space to write a prayer, if they would like to.

If you have any children in your group who want to know more about the good news of Jesus, you could spend some time chatting about it. You might wish to have the booklets detailed on the inside front cover handy to help children think more about becoming friends with God.

Ask the children what Bare Feet's expedition item was today. The compass shows where we are and reminds us that we can serve God wherever we are, we are never too near or far. Show the children your compass and put it in your rucksack with the clothes and the snacks from the previous sessions.

With all ages

- Do you have any questions about what it means to be friends with Jesus?
- If you are already friends with Jesus, how would you tell someone else about him?

Talk with the children about what sort of difference Philip made to the world. What sort of Kingdom Footprint did Philip leave? Come up with a phrase and write it on a large footprint shape. Stick the paper to a cane/stick and take your 'flag' to the expedition debrief. There is also space in both the **Travel Log** and **Expedition Log** to write or draw today's Kingdom Footprint.

Radio transmission

Explain that an easy way to pray is to praise God for how amazing he is, to say sorry for something, to thank God for something and to ask God about something. Encourage the children to practise praying, if they want to. Use the following sentence starters and invite the children to fill in the blanks with their own words before

you move onto the next one. You can do this all together as a group and just let everyone say what they want to before moving on to the next bit.

**We praise you, God, that you are…
I am sorry, God, for…
Thank you, God, for…
God, I want to ask you…
Amen.**

Remind the children that God talks to us as well, so we need to listen as well as speak when we are praying!

Construction

Choose a construction activity from pages 70 to 73. There are two types of construction: *Polar Explorer* constructions that follow the theme of the club and can be done on any day, and Bible constructions that link with each Expedition's Bible teaching. Today's Bible construction is 'Chariot craft' on page 73.

For more craft ideas, see *Ultimate Craft* (SU 978 1 84427 364 5).

Games

Help the Explorers shape up by choosing suitable games from page 74 to 76. For more games ideas, see *Ultimate Games* (SU 978 1 84427 365 2).

Expedition debrief
25 minutes all together

Reporting back

In their exploration time, each team will have explored what Philip's Kingdom Footprint was. As in yesterday's reporting back time, Sir Random invites a couple of children to come and show their team's footprint and puts the information onto his own footprint.

Uploaded data stream

Choose a few jokes, pictures and messages from the data stream. Answer any questions that have been put into the stream. Encourage everyone to carry on uploading their contributions!

Dancing on ice

The band, Poles Apart, lead the children in a couple of lively songs.

Drama: *The Ice Adventure*

Introduce the next episode of the drama. The team have lost all their equipment down a crevasse in the ice. They think all is lost until Helen travels off and finds a store of everything they need left behind by another expedition.

Radio scan

Say that God wants everyone in the world to know him and be part of his big expedition. Either put up a picture of a world map or have a large one on the floor that people can gather round. Invite a few of the leaders to tell brief stories about people they know in different places on the map who are part of God's big expedition. Make sure you include some people in your own country so that the children understand that they don't have to travel a long way to tell others about Jesus. Say that these people were willing to trust God to go anywhere to tell people about Jesus. Pray for the people mentioned now, thanking God that they were willing to do what he wanted and asking that they would leave big Kingdom Footprints. Explain that the children can say 'Amen' at the end if they agree with your prayer. Say that we sometimes close our eyes when we pray so that we can concentrate and not get distracted by those around us. Say that even if a child doesn't want to concentrate on praying, it's nice to remain still and quiet to respect those who do.

When you've finished, tell the children that they can talk to their Huskies if they want to know more about being friends with Jesus.

Into the unknown

Play a game of musical places. Write the names of local and distant places on A4 sheets of paper, enough for two or three less than the number of children, and scatter them around an open space. Ask Poles Apart to play some music; when the music stops challenge the children to stand on a place name. Any children who can't find a place to stand on are out. Play several rounds, taking away two or three place names each time, until you have a winner.

Data upload

Remind the children of today's *Key data*. Summarise the key points of the story and remind the children that the effect we have on the world when we do what God asks us is like leaving Kingdom Footprints. Ask the children to remind you of the third thing that we need to help us on an expedition (compass to show us where we are). The compass helps us to remember that we can serve God anywhere.

Sir Random Finds reminds everyone about the collection procedure and says he is looking forward to seeing everyone next time when we'll go on another mini-expedition and see what sort of Kingdom Footprint another character from the Bible left on the world. He then sends the children back to their team HQs.

. . . .

Over and out
10 minutes

Look at a map of your area. See if the children can find where they live on it. Use a compass to discover which direction they have to travel to get home. If you have any time left, you can complete some of the sections from the **EXPEDITION LOG** or **TRAVEL LOG**, continue with a construction project or just chat together about the day.

Make sure you are available to talk to any children who want to respond to what they have heard today.

. . . .

Husky situation report
30 minutes

Once the children have gone, try to have a debrief as soon as is possible – What went well? What didn't work quite as it should have? Are there any individual issues that the team need to be aware of? Get the expedition leaders to briefly share how their team is doing. Pray together and remember to encourage and affirm each team member in their role. Make sure that any set up or preparation for the next day, or the next club session, is done before you release the team!

EXPEDITION 4
Never Too Bad
TO BE PART OF GOD'S BIG EXPEDITION

For three-day clubs, miss out EXPEDITION 4.

For a four-day club: summarise the story of Philip at the beginning of *Adventure tales*, before you tell the children about Saul.

In Expeditions 1 and 2, we learnt about two of Jesus' friends and how they told everyone about what Jesus had done. And we heard what their message was – Jesus took the punishment for all the bad stuff in our lives, so that we can be friends with God again.

The book of Acts in the Bible tells about lots of Jesus' friends – two of them were Philip and Saul. Philip was one of Jesus' 12 disciples. He was so excited about telling people what Jesus had done for them that he went wherever God told him. God told him to find a man from Ethiopia and tell him about Jesus – and that's exactly what he did. And the Ethiopian man became a friend of Jesus! Wherever you are you can be part of God's big expedition! Today we are going to find out about Saul and that you can never be too bad to be part of God's big expedition.

Explorers' background

No church background

Children may know the story of Saul from RE lessons at school. This is a story of a complete turn around. Saul had been responsible for killing and imprisoning Christians and yet God not only accepts him, he transforms his life and Saul ends up writing half of the New Testament! It is unlikely that children this age will have done truly wicked and evil things, but it is hoped that they will see that no one is beyond the love of God and the possibility of transformation.

Church children

Church children will almost certainly know this story but it may be that they have heard it so many times that it doesn't really make an impact anymore. They need to understand just how bad Saul had been – this is the guy that shared the huge responsibility for Stephen's murder – and many more. Saul was a bona fide enemy of Jesus and his church but suddenly he becomes one of its major leaders and one of the most remembered people in the early church. God calls us to be open to the possibility of major life transformation, even among those who seem to be a long way from God.

Other faiths

Only Judaism, Christianity and Hinduism of contemporary major faiths include theophanic (God appearing) stories. Most Jews and Hindus do not believe that God or gods still appear today. Some Christians, but not all, do. Other faiths do accept that people can have visions, as Ananias does here, so it may be useful to emphasise Saul's physical encounter, leading to blindness.

Prayer is integral to all faith groups, but there may be questions about how Ananias and Saul 'hear' God. See *Top Tips on Prompting Prayer* for help with that (SU 978 1 84427 322 5).

The other faiths strive for people to choose to live differently, better. Only in Christianity is forgiveness offered and reconciliation with God possible for those who still sin, with repentance the only condition. Saul responds to what God asks of him; he doesn't change because he suddenly changes his mind.

Additional needs

Greet all the children by name and with welcoming smiles, especially any who needed a little redirection on the previous day. Unsettled behaviour is sometimes a cry for attention. Give them positive attention, check how they are feeling, there may be a difficulty at home that prompted unwanted behaviours at the event.

Children who have Down syndrome often struggle to read but love music and echo others' words or sign. You might consider drawing out the memory verse with symbols or pictures so that a non- or emergent reader will be able to 'read' the pictures and begin to memorise the verse.

EXPEDITION 4 **preparation**

Key character and passage
Saul – Acts 9:1–31

Key storylines
- Saul had been one of the key enemies of Jesus and his followers – he'd even had Christians killed.
- Jesus met Saul on the road to Damascus; Saul spent the rest of his life following Jesus and sharing his good news.
- We need to have a map to help us navigate on our expedition.

Key aims
- To welcome the children back to the club.
- To help the children understand that God doesn't let what we have been prevent us from being part of his big expedition.
- To help the children continue to explore that we are never too *anything* for God to use us. Today the children will see that God can turn any life around – even those who might think they're beyond his reach.
- To help the children discover Saul's Kingdom Footprint.

Husky time
Spiritual preparation
Invite the team to come up with a list of people who some might think are truly wicked and evil. Encourage them to talk about the atrocities they have committed. Get a real feel for how bad people can be. Ask the team to try and put their knowledge of the following story on hold for a few minutes. Imagine they are coming to it fresh, for the first time.

Read Acts 8:1–3 and Acts 9:1,2.

Ask for words to describe Saul. It needs to come out that this man was not a good guy!

Read Acts 9:3–9.

Ask for their honest responses to what God does in these verses. Does Saul deserve to have a second chance? Try and free people up to be really honest and not just give the right Christian answers!

Read Acts 9:10–19.

What must this whole episode have felt like for Ananias? Encourage everyone to imagine how conflicted he might have felt. It might be useful to come up with a list of words that could describe Ananias' emotions.

Ask the team to tell you what they know of Saul's significance in church history after this point. What did he do? What do we remember him for? Did his good ever make up for his bad? Is that possible or is that a bogus concept?

Spend some time praying for the children who will come to the club, that they will realise that they are not too bad to be loved and welcomed by God.

Practical preparation
Talk through the programme, making sure that everyone understands the activities and has the resources to deliver them if necessary. Check that the team are feeling comfortable and enabled.

Point out that in today's Bible passage the character is known as Saul rather than Paul. The DVD and session material use this name. Ask team members to be careful in their use of the name, so as not to confuse the children, but to be ready to respond to children who do know about the dual name.

Set up all the different areas in the club, making sure you are ready for when the first children arrive. Ensure that any activities from the previous expedition are well displayed both in the team HQs and at the front, as appropriate. You might like to have Sir Random Finds and Bare Feet wandering around in character speaking to the children as they arrive.

WHAT-YOU-NEED CHECKLIST
- [ ] **Registration**: registration forms, badges, labels, pens, expedition team lists
- [ ] **Expedition team leaders**: Bibles, **Travel Logs** or **Expedition Logs**, large sheet of paper (lining paper is ideal), felt-tip pens, rucksack and map for 5 to 8s groups, a large blank footprint.
- [ ] **Basic training**: two full sets of clothes
- [ ] **Data report**: whiteboard for ongoing list of things needed for an expedition, a digital camera and the means to print photos during session
- [ ] **Technology**: PA system, projection system for Power Points, song words, etc, **Polar Explorers** DVD
- [ ] **Music**: Poles Apart band or backing tracks
- [ ] **Drama**: costumes and props
- [ ] **Activities**: equipment for games and construction
- [ ] **Sir Random and Bare Feet**: running order, big sheet of paper and marker pen, *Learn and remember* verse
- [ ] **Adventure tales: Polar Explorers** DVD (or the story script, boo/hiss and cheer cards)
- [ ] **Key data**: whiteboard for ongoing list of key data
- [ ] **Uploaded data stream box**: a selection of jokes, messages and pictures
- [ ] **Refuelling station**: drinks and snacks
- [ ] **Photographer**: digital camera

EXPEDITION 4 **programme**

Do you copy?
10 minutes

Be ready to welcome your children back to their expedition team. Ask the children what they did after **POLar EXPLorers** last time and what they are looking forward to in today's session.

You can use this time to continue to decorate your team area. Today you could work together to produce a map of an imaginary wilderness on a large sheet of paper to display. You could include features such as forests, lakes, deserts, oases, mountains and cliffs. You might include a solitary road running through your wilderness. As you work, chat together about what they think of the club so far. What questions do they have? Has anyone thought more about becoming a friend of Jesus?

Base camp
45 minutes all together

Situation report
Sir Random Finds and Bare Feet come on, setting the tone for the session. By this time they will have quite a lot of material to chat about – perhaps some shared jokes about something that has happened earlier in the club. It's really just to say 'Hello!'

Sir Random Finds reminds the children about God's big expedition: how Jesus' friends go out to help other people to start being friends of Jesus too. On today's mini-expedition they will find out about an… enemy of Jesus called Saul.

Basic training
Unveil your two sets of explorers' clothes in piles at the front. Look at the leader board and comment on who has done well so far at **POLar EXPLorers**. This time ask two children to race to get dressed in all the gear, and encourage them to be faster than the Huskies. Use a stopwatch to record the times and put today's contestants on the leader board.

Data report
Sir Random Finds looks at the *Data checklist* and reminds the children that it shows the things that will help Bare Feet on her expedition.

Sir Random and Bare Feet continue to chat about the idea of the carbon footprint. Sir Random is *still* getting mixed up with this. Bare Feet is keen to explore a particular part of the wilderness today. She has had her breakfast and has the right clothes on for her expedition. She also has the enormous compass on a cord hanging around her neck. Sir Random asks her where exactly she'll be going. Bare Feet doesn't know exactly but she has a compass, so she's sure she will be fine! Sir Random tells Bare Feet that a compass is a great start but you need a map to use it in the best way. A map shows you exactly where something is and the sorts of things you'll pass on the way there. A map can tell you how much further you have to go.

Sir Random further explains how a map works by drawing a big map of their base. Bare Feet practises using the map to find her way around the various features of the room. There can be a bit of interplay here about Sir Random's bad drawing and what Bare Feet might mistakenly think she's looking for. Sir Random could also bring in the idea of a Sat Nav and direct her round the room in the style of a Sat Nav. (In 300 metres, turn left, turn left now, you missed the turn, recalculating route etc.)

Sir Random Finds writes 'Map for information' on Bare Feet's *Data checklist* of things to help her. He could also take a photo of Bare Feet with her map. This can be printed during the club and be put up for the *Expedition debrief* section. Bare Feet heads out into the wild.

Dancing on ice
The band, Poles Apart, lead the children in the **POLar EXPLorers** theme song.

Message from base
Sir Random tells one of his stories:

Did I ever tell you about the time when I was going to Iceland on a trip? Not Iceland that your mum goes to for sausage rolls and frozen peas, but Iceland with the volcanoes. I was so looking forward to that trip with a nice team. And then we heard that another chap was coming with us. He was a bad lad alright, a real criminal. He'd even been in prison. I didn't want him to come at all. But do you know, I was totally wrong! It turns out he'd done a lot of thinking in prison and wanted to change his ways. He did a super job on the team and now he takes boys on expeditions who've been expelled from school. In fact, that reminds me of a story about someone in the Bible…

Adventure tales
Introduce the **POLar EXPLorers** DVD. In today's episode, Gemma and Blizz are relieved to be back in the cabin after getting lost in a blizzard. They talk about how sometimes we can feel lost even when we know where we are. Gemma tells the story of Saul to show that, however lost we seem to be, God will always help us find our way.

If you have a talented storyteller on your team, you may wish to also tell the children the story. Either use the fully scripted retold Bible story for Expedition 4 on the **POLar EXPLorers** website or the storyteller could tell the story based on Acts 9:1–31 using their own words if possible. You can use the section headings and interactive ideas from the script as memory joggers and to vary your story presentation each time.

If you are telling the story as well as using the DVD, tell the story first, then show the DVD so the children already have the outline of the events before seeing the episode.

Key data
Sir Random Finds then helps the children think about today's story using the key phrase 'Never too bad to be part of God's big expedition':

EXPEDITION 4

Saul had done some really bad things – he wanted to put all the Christians in prison because they didn't believe the same thing he did! But his 'badness' didn't stop God wanting Saul as a part of his big expedition. He completely changed Saul's life with that meeting on the road to Damascus.

Maybe you're thinking, 'I've been too bad to be friends with Jesus. There's no way that God would want me on his expedition.' Well, you're wrong – he does! There's nothing we can do to stop God loving us and wanting us to be his friend. Maybe you want to talk about this more? Then chat with your Huskies!

Write the phrase, **'Never too bad to be part of God's big expedition'** on your *Key data board*.

Hear from the Husky
Bare Feet asks a leader to come up and share a story about someone they know who went from being really bad to having a part in God's story. If no one has a story like this, you could find a story of someone who turned away from a bad life towards God. Someone like Nicky Cruz, perhaps.

Bare Feet can say she was glad that Sir Random made her take the map today. It really helped her to know exactly where she was and where she was headed to. The Bible is a bit like a map because it shows us the way to be a friend of Jesus.

Learn and remember
Have sets of the letters for the word 'peace', enough for one per team. Give each team a set of letters, and see which one can work out the word the fastest.

Say that Saul was an enemy of God and there are lots of people who are enemies of God, but Jesus wants everyone to be a friend of God. Explain that when people become friends we say that they are at peace with each other. Ask the children if they can remember how the word peace fits into the *Learn and remember* verse. Display the whole verse on the screen and get everyone to read it out together.

'Wear shoes that are able to speed you on as you preach the Good News of peace with God'
Ephesians 6:15 (Living Bible).

There's also a song, 'Speedy shoes', on the **POLaR EXPLOReRS** website and DVD to help the children to learn the verse.

● ● ● ● ● ● ● ● ● ● ● ● ● ● ● ● ● ● ● ●

Expedition time
45 minutes in small groups

Refuelling station
Make sure the children are comfortable in their team HQs as the Huskies help them with refreshments. Give children the opportunity to use the toilet. Younger children can take a long time over snack, so you may choose to begin your discussion as they are eating and drinking.

Bible exploration
With older children (8 to 11s)

Ask the children to tell you about some 'baddies' from films or TV programmes. What makes them so bad? What kind of things do they do? There is space to draw a favourite 'baddie' on page 29 of the **EXPeDITION LOG**.

Read the two short passages on page 30 together – they are from Acts 8:1–3 and Acts 9:1,2 (make sure the children understand that these words are from the Bible). Talk about the bad things that Saul was doing. Remind the children that these are things that actually happened, not just events in a movie or TV programme. Why would God choose to use a person as bad as this? Challenge the group to think of any fictional 'baddies' who become 'goodies'.

Ask the group to use the Bible verses referenced to draw pictures of the next part of Saul's story in the photo spaces on pages 31 to 33.

Say that Saul was also known as Paul and he wrote lots of letters to lots of Jesus' followers in many different places. We still have 13 of these letters in the Bible.

Ask the group if they can remember what Bare Feet's essential item was today. What does a map do? A

map's job is to show you how to get somewhere. The Bible is a bit like a map because it shows us the way to be a friend of Jesus. We have used the Bible today to discover several different things – encourage the group to think how. God gave us the Bible so that we would be able to follow him well. One of the ways we can use it well is to read it regularly. Say that the stories in **POLaR EXPLOReRS** about people who were friends of Jesus are from the Bible, and each day they have been reading bits of the Bible in their **EXPeDITION LOG**. (If your club has the budget, it might be good to give the children their own set of age-appropriate daily Bible reading guides at this point.)

Our *Learn and remember* verse is from one of the letters Paul wrote. How much of the verse can the group remember? If they haven't yet done so, they can use the code cracker to discover the verse on pages 4 and 5 of the **EXPeDITION LOG**.

With younger children (5 to 8s)

Invite the children to draw some of their favourite fictional 'baddies' on page 18 of the **TRaVeL LOG**. Talk about what makes a 'baddie' bad. Who was a 'baddie' to start with in today's story? Encourage the children to think of any fictional characters who started as 'baddies' but turned into 'goodies'? Did today's 'baddie' turn into a 'goodie'?

Read the story again to the children from Acts 9:1–20. (Read the start of the story on page 19.) Encourage the children to point to the right pictures on page 20 as you tell the whole story. Afterwards, see if the children can tell one another the story using the pictures as prompts.

Chat for a moment about the big change in Saul's life. Remind them that Jesus' good news is for everyone, even people who have done terrible things, like Saul. Say that no one has been too naughty to be loved by God.

Say that using these pictures to help us is a bit like having a map of the story. Bare Feet needed a map today, didn't she? The Bible can be a bit like a map, too, because it shows us how to to be a friend of Jesus by telling us stories and giving instructions. Show the group your map and put it in the rucksack with the other equipment.

With all ages

- How would you describe Saul?
- Can people be 'too bad' to follow Jesus?
- If you were Ananias, how would you have felt about meeting Saul?

Talk with the children about what sort of difference Saul made to the world – what was his Kingdom Footprint? Come up with a phrase and write it on a large footprint shape. There is also space in both the **TRAVEL LOG** and **EXPEDITION LOG** to write or draw today's Kingdom Footprints.

Radio transmission

Remind the children that, after Saul had become a friend of Jesus, he wrote letters to help other people be a friend of Jesus and part of God's big expedition. These letters are part of the Bible.

Have a plate of tea lights and a taper for each team, with someone to supervise each plate. Encourage the children, one at a time in each team, to come up and light a tea light either for someone they know to become a friend of Jesus or for themselves to know Jesus better. (It's fine if some children don't want to do this, they can just watch.) When everyone who wants to has lit their light, say a brief prayer for everyone represented by the lights. At the end say: 'Amen – 1, 2, 3…' and all blow out the lights together.

Construction

Choose a construction activity from pages 70 to 73. There are two types of construction: **Polar Explorer** constructions that follow the theme of the club and can be done on any day, and Bible constructions that link with each Expedition's Bible teaching. Today's Bible construction is 'Forgiveness stones' on page 73.

For more craft ideas, see *Ultimate Craft* (SU 978 1 84427 364 5).

Games

Help the explorers shape up by choosing suitable games from page 74 to 76. For more games

ideas, see *Ultimate Games* (SU 978 1 84427 365 2).

Expedition debrief
25 minutes all together

Reporting back

In their exploration time, each team will have discovered what the Kingdom Footprint was for Saul. As in yesterday's reporting back time, Sir Random invites a couple of children to come and show their team's footprint and puts the information onto his own footprint.

Uploaded data stream

Select some jokes, pictures and messages from the data stream. Answer any questions that have been put into the stream. Encourage everyone to carry on uploading their contributions – there's only one day left!

Dancing on ice

The band, Poles Apart, lead the children in a couple of lively songs.

Drama: *The Ice Adventure*

Introduce the next episode of the drama. Great Scott is furious that the expedition is still carrying on, despite his attempts to sabotage it. And then he is discovered to be a fraud.

Radio scan

Ask the children to think of stories they have heard in the news where people have done really bad things. Say that God loves those people even though they did terrible things and he wants them to be part of his big expedition. Pray together that God would help those people come to know him. Explain that the children can say 'Amen' at the end if they agree with your prayer. Say that we sometimes close our eyes when we pray so that we can concentrate and not get distracted by those around us. Say that even if a child doesn't want to concentrate on praying, it's nice to remain still and quiet to respect those that do.

Into the unknown

Create a map of your venue with particular spots marked on it, like an orienteering course. At each spot, have a small prize hidden. Invite volunteers to go and retrieve the prize from one of the marked spots.

Data upload

Remind the children of today's *Key data*. Summarise the key points of the story and remind the children that the effect we have on the world when we do what God asks us is like leaving Kingdom Footprints. Ask the children to remind you what the fourth thing was that we need to help us on an expedition (map for information).

Sir Random Finds reminds everyone about the collection procedure and says he is looking forward to seeing everyone next time when we'll go on another mini-expedition and see what sort of Kingdom Footprint another character from the Bible left on the world. He then sends the children back to their team HQs.

Over and out
10 minutes small groups

In your final team time of the session, challenge the children to see if they can write directions for how to get home. Alternatively, you could try to find routes on a map to places in your town (the library, town hall or local park).

If you have time, finish anything off that you ran out of time for earlier – your construction project, pages from the **TRAVEL LOGS** or **EXPEDITION LOGS** or your wilderness map. As you work, chat together about the day – what did the children enjoy? What questions do they have about what they've experienced?

Make sure you are available to talk to any children who want to respond to what they have heard today.

Husky situation report
30 minutes

Once the children have gone, try to have a debrief as soon as is possible – what went well? What didn't work quite as it should have? Are there any individual issues that the team need to be aware of? Invite the expedition leaders to briefly share how their team is doing. Pray together and remember to encourage and affirm each team member in their role. Make sure that any set up or preparation for the next day (or the next time the club will meet) is done before you release the team!

EXPEDITION 5
never too young
TO Be ParT Of GOD's BIG exPeDITION

EXPEDITION 5 **should be included for** *all* **clubs.**

If you wish, summarise the stories from EXPEDITIONS **3 and** 4 **at the start of** *Adventure tales*:

The book of Acts in the Bible tells about lots of Jesus' friends – two of them were Philip and Paul. Philip was one of Jesus' 12 disciples. He was so excited about telling people what Jesus had done for them that he went wherever God told him. God told him to go a long way to find a man from Ethiopia and tell him about Jesus – and that's exactly what he did. And the Ethiopian man became a friend of Jesus! You're never too near or far to be part of God's big expedition!

Paul wasn't one of Jesus' friends at the start – in fact he hated Jesus and wanted to cause trouble for his friends. However, while he was on the way to arrest some friends of Jesus, he saw a great light, which blinded him. Jesus started to talk to him and told him he had to change his ways. With the help of a man called Ananias, Paul said he was sorry and started to tell people how amazing Jesus is. You're never too bad to be part of God's big expedition!

Then continue with Expedition 5's story.

Explorers' **background**

No church background
Timothy probably isn't a character that children from outside church will know, so be careful not to assume knowledge.

There is not a nice neat story about Timothy to share, but rather a collection of points about his character. Children are often told, 'You're too young to do that' and they can end up feeling like they can't do anything exciting, important or useful until they grow up.

Non church children will not be thinking about how they can serve God in a church context, but they need to know that they can be a friend of Jesus and tell others about Jesus whatever their age.

Church children
Not too many churches encourage children to take an active part in the life of the church in terms of serving in ministry settings, and it's important for them to hear that their young age needn't be a barrier to them being part of God's story. Timothy was encouraged not to be frightened or timid but rather to rely on God for a spirit of power, love and self-discipline. Church children may be excited by this possibility!

Other faiths
All faiths expect parents to raise their children to worship and live according to the faith. Muslim or Buddhist children may ask about Timothy's father. Emphasise that describing dad as 'Greek' implies 'not Jewish', so he

couldn't have passed on that faith. Being circumcised was an outward sign of being Jewish, which Timothy was. Jewish and Muslim boys might connect with that.

Mohammed was first supported by young men, and Buddha was a young man, so young age should not be an issue for Muslims or Buddhists.

For Christians, salvation and calling come from our response to the grace of God. This is similar to the view of Jews and Muslims. However, in those faiths, good works must outweigh evil deeds to prove one is worthy. Sikhs, Jains and Hindus see salvation in escaping the cycle of reincarnation and strive for a state of bliss similar to the Nirvana sought in Buddhism – being part of a universal 'nothingness'.

Additional needs
Now that the children are all feeling more confident it would be a good day to look for 'buddy pairings'; non-disabled children who would enjoy and learn from the role of supporting another child in their expedition team who has an additional need. It will be a great way to demonstrate 'never too young'. If the child being supported has no use of his or her voice, there is a lovely opportunity for their buddy to record something that might want to be said. They could use a simple switch that allows up to 10 seconds of speech to be recorded (see www.inclusive.co.uk).

EXPEDITION 5 **preparation**

Key character and passages

Timothy – Acts 16; 1 Timothy 4; 2 Timothy 1

Key storylines

- Timothy was a young disciple who had been brought up by godly family.
- Timothy, despite his youth, had great character and was picked by two of the church's major players (Paul and Silas) to go on mission with them.
- We need to have a way of recording information to help us remember the key points from our expedition.

Key aims

- To welcome the children to the club.
- To help the children understand that God doesn't let our young age get in the way of us being part of his big expedition.
- To explore Timothy's story and see how he worked for God.
- To help children uncover Timothy's Kingdom Footprint.

Husky time

Spiritual preparation

Ask the team to get themselves in order of age. Make small groups of people in a similar life-stage – under-18s, 18 to 25s, 25 to 35s, 35 to 50s, 50 to 65s, over-65s. Feel free to amalgamate groups according to the size of your team. Ask the small groups to come up with some positive things about being at their life-stage and some negative things. Have some brief feedback between groups.

Read 1 Timothy 4:6–16 and 2 Timothy 1:3–8.

What do we learn about Timothy from these passages? Why is it difficult to be a leader when you are young? What benefits does it have?

Read Acts 16:1–5.

Why do you think Paul and Silas chose Timothy to go with them? What sort of qualities should we look for in those who we call to lead?

Go back to 2 Timothy 1:6,7. Ask the team what spiritual gifts they feel they have been given. Encourage them to talk in twos or threes and then pray for one another, that God would fan these gifts into flame and that they would have a spirit of power, love and self-discipline. (Be aware of team members who are not comfortable with small group activities and offer an alternative.)

Pray for the children, that even though they are young, they would know and experience God using them in amazing ways.

Practical preparation

Talk through the programme, making sure that everyone understands the activities and has the resources to deliver them if necessary. Check that the team are feeling comfortable and enabled.

Point out that Saul from Expedition 4 has had his name changed to Paul. Encourage team members to make sure that their children understand that this is the same person.

Try not to pack anything away during the session. Though this might make things easier for you at the end of this last day, it will make the children feel uncomfortable, as if the club is coming to a premature end.

Set up all the different areas in the club, making sure you are ready for when the first children arrive. Ensure that any activities from previous expeditions are well displayed both in the team HQs and at the front, as appropriate. You might like to have Sir Random Finds and Bare Feet wandering around in character speaking to the children as they arrive.

WHAT-YOU-NEED CHECKLIST

- [ ] **Registration**: registration forms, badges, labels, pens, expedition team lists
- [ ] **Expedition team leaders**: photo-sized pieces of card, Bibles, **TRAVEL LOGS** or **EXPEDITION LOGS**, large paper, felt-tip pens, rucksack and travel journal for 5 to 8s groups, a large blank footprint
- [ ] **Basic training**: two full sets of clothes, stopwatch
- [ ] **Data report**: whiteboard for ongoing list of things needed for an expedition, a large camera
- [ ] **Technology**: PA system, projection system for PowerPoints, song words etc, **POLAR EXPLORERS** DVD
- [ ] **Music**: Poles Apart band or backing tracks
- [ ] **Drama**: costumes and props
- [ ] **Activities**: equipment for games and construction
- [ ] **Sir Random and Bare Feet**: running order, *Learn and remember* verse, large map, footprint shapes cut from coloured paper
- [ ] **Adventure tales**: **POLAR EXPLORERS** DVD (or the story script, storytelling volunteers, props and costumes)
- [ ] **Key data**: whiteboard for ongoing list of key data
- [ ] **Uploaded data stream box**: a selection of jokes, messages and pictures
- [ ] **Refuelling station**: drinks and snacks
- [ ] **Photographer**: digital camera

EXPEDITION 5 **programme**

Do you copy?
10 minutes in small groups

Be ready to welcome your children back to their team. Ask what the children remember from the week at **POLar EXPLorers** and what they have done since the previous club session.

You can use this time to start to draw your thoughts and findings together. Ask the children to imagine they could take a photograph of something they've remembered or seen at **POLar EXPLorers**. Give them photo-sized pieces of paper or card (10 cm x 15 cm) and encourage them to draw their imaginary photo. You might like to peg these onto a string somewhere in your area. You could also encourage the children to finish off anything that remains undone from previous expeditions. As you work, chat about the things that have made the biggest impression on the children.

Base camp
45 minutes all together

Situation report
Sir Random Finds and Bare Feet come on, setting the tone for the session as they have done throughout the club.

Sir Random Finds reminds the children about God's big expedition: how Jesus' friends go out to help other people to start being friends of Jesus too. On today's mini-expedition they will find out about a friend of Jesus called Timothy.

Basic training
Show your two sets of explorers' clothes in piles at the front. Look at the leader board and comment on who has done well so far at **POLar EXPLorers**. Ask two Junior Huskies to race to get dressed in all the gear. Use a stopwatch to record the times and put today's contestants on the leader board. If you're not having a closing service, announce the *Basic training* winner!

Data report
Sir Random Finds looks at the *Data checklist* and reminds the children that it shows the things that will help Bare Feet on her expedition.

Sir Random has just about got his head round the idea of carbon footprints today. Bare Feet is keen to start drawing her thoughts from her expeditions together – she has had her breakfast and has the right clothes on for her expedition. She also has the enormous compass on a cord hanging around her neck, plus a map pouch or GPS device. Sir Random asks her how she will draw her findings together. Bare Feet hasn't really thought about that. She just thinks she'll go out and have another quick look at things.

Sir Random suggests that she might want to find a way of remembering her information. He muses, if only there were a way of storing pictures of everything you've seen… There can be some interplay between him and the children about what could do such a job. They will realise that a digital camera would be just the thing. Sir Random gives Bare Feet a camera – a big toy one would be ideal.

Sir Random Finds continues the *Data checklist* for Bare Feet to remember what she needs on an expedition – he should write on it 'Data storage device'. He could also take a photo of Bare Feet with her camera. This can be printed during the club and be put up for the *Expedition debrief* section. Bare Feet heads out into the wild.

Dancing on ice
The band, Poles Apart, lead the children in the **POLar EXPLorers** theme song.

Message from base
Sir Random tells one of his stories:

Did I ever tell you about the first trip I ever went on? Well I was frightfully young. Hardly even out of school, but I was enormously enthusiastic. I had read so many books and been on so many training camps and expeditions. But, you know, the explorers' world is all about age and experience and I was far too young to have a shot at anything big. Then, out of nowhere, I got an invitation to take part in the most smashing adventure with a very famous explorer at the time. It

was the making of me – I couldn't believe they would take a chance on someone so young and inexperienced, but they did, and it made me the man I am today. In fact, that reminds me of a story about someone in the Bible…

Adventure tales
Introduce the **POLar EXPLorers** DVD. Today, Blizz realises that he's not too young to be a polar explorer because God has created him with everything he needs for the job! Gemma explains that we are never too young to start following Jesus either, and tells him the story of Timothy. Inspired, they set off on another adventure!

If you have a talented storyteller on your team, you may wish to also tell the children the story. Either use the fully scripted retold Bible story for Expedition 5 on the **POLar EXPLorers** website or the storyteller could tell the story based on Acts 16; 1 Timothy 4; 2 Timothy 1 using their own words if possible. You can use the section headings and interactive ideas from the script as memory joggers and to vary your story presentation each time.

If you are telling the story as well as using the DVD, tell the story first, then show the DVD so the children already have the outline of the events before seeing the episode.

Key data
Sir Random Finds then helps the children to think about today's story using the key phrase 'Never too young to be part of God's big expedition':

Timothy was a young man who went on some amazing adventures! He was ready to follow Jesus and went with Paul on God's big expedition. At the start of his adventures, he was a young man, but that didn't stop him! He did some great things for God.

There are times when we don't get to do things because we're too young, and sometimes that's sensible, because they are too dangerous or difficult for us. But there are plenty of things that we can do. For starters, we're never too young to say yes to Jesus – to say yes,

I want to be friends with God. And we're never too young to be part of what God is doing – to tell others about Jesus, to help people, to show others how much God loves them.

Do you want to say yes to Jesus? Do you want to tell others about him? Do you want to do things which show people how much God loves them? You can do all of these things!

Write the phrase **'Never too young to be part of God's big expedition'** on your *Key data board*.

Hear from the Husky

Bare Feet asks a leader to come up and share a story about doing something amazing for God when they were still quite young. They can talk about people who encouraged them when they were young.

Bare Feet can say she was glad that Sir Random made her take the camera today, she's got lots of really good pictures to support her research. It can be a great idea to write down important things that we learn about God and stories of things that he does in our lives. Sometimes we might even write letters or emails to other Christians to encourage them – just like Paul did for Timothy.

Learn and remember

Display a large map of your town or area. Invite the children to come and scatter footprint shapes across the map where they may want to tell people about Jesus. Say the *Learn and remember* verse together:

'Wear shoes that are able to speed you on as you preach the Good News of peace with God' Ephesians 6:15 (Living Bible).

There's also a song, 'Speedy shoes', on the **POLar EXPLOrers** website and DVD to help the children to learn the verse.

Expedition time
45 minutes in small groups

Refuelling station

Make sure the children are comfortable in their team HQs as the Huskies help them with refreshments. Give children the opportunity to use the toilet.

Younger children can take a long time over snack, so you may choose to begin your discussion as they eat and drink.

Bible exploration
With older children (8 to 11s)

Remind the children of the characters we saw in today's story and the good things they had to say about Timothy. Ask the children to write down in the speech bubbles (page 36 of the **EXPEDITION LOG**) good things that people say (or that they would like people to say) about them. An alternative way to do this is to have the children pass their books around the group so that they can all write positive things about one another (but this needs careful supervision to watch for unhelpful comments!).

Read the passage from 1 Timothy 4:11–16 on page 37 of the **EXPEDITION LOG**. Talk about why people might have struggled with Timothy being so young. Ask the group to think about what sorts of things they can't do when they are young. Now look back through the passage and see what Paul tells Timothy he can do. Can we do these things too? Invite the children to pull out key words from the passage and write them decoratively on page 39. See if they can make the words look like their meanings.

Ask the children what Bare Feet's expedition item was today. She had a camera, but the idea was a way to record the data she had collected. As we follow Jesus, it can be really good to keep a record of what we are learning and the things that God says to us. We might call this a journal. The **EXPEDITION LOG** has been a kind of journal for us during **POLar EXPLOrers**. Ask the children if they have any hopes or dreams about what they might do for God just now and as they get older.

Finally, invite the children to spend a few minutes writing themselves an encouraging email, as if from Paul. It would be great if you could have written each child an encouraging note or card, which you can give them after they have written their own email (page 40).

With younger children (5 to 8s)

Invite the children to sit in a circle and give one child a small object to hold (it can be anything). While that child is

holding the object, encourage everyone else to say one nice thing about them. Then invite them to pass the object to the next child in the circle and again invite everyone to say something nice, until each child has had a turn holding the object. If possible, write the nice comments down on a separate page for each child, which can later be stuck in their **Travel LOG**. Alternatively, write the things directly onto page 22 of the **Travel LOG** for each child.

Ask the children what they can remember about the things that today's characters said about Timothy. Read some of the words from 2 Timothy from page 23. Say that Timothy was young when he first met Paul and Silas and they took him on their journey. That was a very exciting thing for a young person to do. What kinds of exciting things might these children do for and with God even though they are still young? Encourage them to draw some of their ideas on page 24 of the **Travel LOG**.

Talk to the children about how it can be really helpful to draw or write down the things that we learn about God and the things that he says to us. You might call this a journal. Bare Feet took a camera with her on her expedition to record her data. We might use a journal to record our data on God's big expedition. Show your journal and put it in the rucksack with the other items. If you have time, get all the items out and see if the children can remember the story behind each of them.

With all ages

- What things have you been told you're too young to do? Why?
- How did you feel?
- What do you think about Timothy?
- How can we do similar things to Timothy in our own lives?

Talk with the children about what sort of difference Timothy made to the world. What was his Kingdom Footprint? Come up with a phrase and write it on a blank footprint shape. There is also space in both the **Travel LOG** and **EXPEDITION LOG** to write or draw today's Kingdom Footprint.

Radio transmission

Paul wrote these words to Timothy in a letter: 'God's Spirit doesn't make cowards out of us. The Spirit gives us power, love, and self-control' (2 Timothy 1:7). Help the children to come up with actions for 'Spirit', 'cowards', 'power', 'love' and 'self-control'. Talk about what those words mean. Use this verse to pray together using the actions:

Father God, thank you that you give us your Spirit so that we are not cowards but instead have your power, love and self-control. Amen.

Construction

Choose a construction activity from pages 70 to 73. There are two types of construction: *Polar Explorer* constructions that follow the theme of the club and can be done on any day, and Bible constructions that link with each Expedition's Bible teaching. Today's Bible construction is 'Life of Timothy comic strip' on page 73.

For more craft ideas, see *Ultimate Craft* (SU 978 1 84427 364 5).

Games

Help the explorers shape up by choosing suitable games from page 74 to 76. For more games ideas, see *Ultimate Games* (SU 978 1 84427 365 2).

Expedition debrief
25 minutes all together

Reporting back

In their exploration time, each team will have uncovered Timothy's Kingdom Footprint. As in previous reporting back time, Sir Random invites a couple of children to come and show their teams' footprints and puts the information onto his own footprint.

Uploaded data stream

Select some jokes, pictures and messages from the data stream. Answer any questions that have been put into the stream. Thank everyone for the contributions during the club – if you are having a concluding service, explain that you will answer any remaining questions then, as well as sharing the best jokes and pictures!

Dancing on ice

The band, Poles Apart, lead the children in a couple of lively songs.

Drama: *The Ice Adventure*

Introduce the next episode of the drama. The team finally arrive at Professor Yvonne Von Evian's shelter, ready to deliver the message they have been carrying. They are surprised to find that the Professor is so young, but she explains that the Chief knew she was ready to do the research, regardless of how old she was.

Radio scan

Ask the children to think about what they hope to do when they get a bit older. Ask them to think about which parts of that they might be able to have a go at or learn about when they are this age. Ask the children to stand up. Pray that God would give the children special gifts to do amazing things for him. Pray that the Holy Spirit would fan these gifts into flame while they are still young. Explain that the children can say 'Amen' at the end if they agree with your prayer. Say that we sometimes close our eyes when we pray so that we can concentrate and not get distracted by those around us. Say that even if a child doesn't want to concentrate on praying, it's nice to remain still and quiet to respect those that do.

Into the unknown

During the club, your photographer will have taken lots of photos of all that is going on in the different parts of the programme. At this point, show some of the photos on the screen and ask if the children can remember what's going on in each picture and what key idea or story it relates to.

Data upload

Remind the children of today's *Key data*. Summarise the story's key points and remind the children that the effect we have on the world when we do what God asks is like leaving Kingdom Footprints. Ask the children to remind you of the fifth thing we need to help us on an expedition (data storage device).

Sir Random Finds reminds everyone about the collection procedure and says he will be really sorry not to see them tomorrow. If you are having a concluding service, he can encourage the children

to come along with their friends and families. He then sends the children back to their team HQs.

Over and out
10 minutes in small groups

Ask the children what they will remember most about **Polar Explorers**. Any children who are not normally in touch with one another might like to swap contact details on their autographs pages in the **Expedition** and **Travel Log** (make sure they have their parents' permission to do so).

Spend some time reviewing what you have done during **Polar Explorers**. Look at the things you have made to decorate your HQ – challenge the children to remember what they were all about. Recap the stories and the 'Never too…' phrases. Check to see if the children can remember the *Learn and remember* verse.

Use any remaining time to complete any pages of the **Travel Logs** or **Expedition Logs** or any unfinished construction projects. Don't forget to remind the children about the service, if you're having one.

Make sure you are available to talk to any children who want to respond to what they have heard today.

Husky situation report
30 minutes

Once the children have gone, spend some time doing the bulk of the clearing up before sitting down as a team together. Ideally, share a meal and talk about the club. You may want to give out evaluation forms or just talk more informally about what has worked well or not so well. Are there any key things to be picked up on for next time? If you are having a concluding service, make sure that everyone knows what they are doing in it, and consider how much of the club decoration you want to leave in place for that service. Thank your team and pray blessing on both them and all the children you've been in contact with during the club. Finish with a time of thanking God for who he is and what he's done.

SERVICE 2
Never too unlikely
TO BE PART OF GOD'S BIG EXPEDITION

Explorers' **background**

No church background

Even though the children will have been to some or all of the holiday club sessions, church will not be quite the same experience! Try to include some of the characters and leaders from the club for continuity and familiarity. Make this service as much a part of the holiday club experience as you can.

Church children

These children are familiar with how church works so surprise them by making it feel like an extension of the holiday club, even though it will naturally be a bit different. Include as many of their favourite things from the club as you can – songs, Sir Random and Bare Feet, your drama characters etc.

Other faiths

In the Eastern religions (Buddhism, Jainism, Hinduism, Sikhism), although there are monks and nuns, only Hinduism has priests. However, many of the worship services are held in homes, and women, as well as men, can lead these.

Judaism and Christianity are similar in that some branches accept women leading worship and heading the faith community, but others do not. Currently in Islam, women can lead women-only meetings, but cannot be Imams who head up a mosque.

Some children from strict Muslim homes may be surprised that Lydia was a successful business woman, but remind them that the Prophet Mohammed's wife Fatima was also a business woman.

Additional needs

This would be a great place for any children that have set up a speech switch between them to demonstrate that by giving feedback or saying a prayer. It could even be simply set up with 'Amen' to give the child the option of agreeing with a prayer that has been said.

The families of the children you have included will be greatly encouraged by your non-judgemental acceptance. Remember that not all children with additional needs have a formal identification of their difficulties. Make friends with them all and discover the stress points in their daily lives. Are there adults in the church that might be family buddies helping with shopping, babysitting, listening or whatever is needed? All you have to do is ask. Continue to pray for each family you have met.

SERVICE 2 **preparation**

Key passage
Acts 16:11–15

Key storylines
- Paul, Silas, Timothy and Luke met Lydia on their journey in a city called Philippi.
- Lydia was important and wealthy – and also a woman – all of which might have made her an unlikely candidate for becoming a Christian.
- Lydia came to faith and, because she was a community leader, many other people came to faith through her.

Key aims
- To hear about many of the different characters who were part of God's big expedition.
- To share with the rest of the church community what's been happening at **POLar EXPLOrers**.

- To welcome any children and their associated adults who have been to the club but who wouldn't usually come to a worship service. The service needs to tread the line between being like the holiday club but also like a service.

WHAT-YOU-NEED CHECKLIST:
- [ ] A PowerPoint of animal footprints
- [ ] A PowerPoint of key figures and *Key data*
- [ ] The reading and a reader
- [ ] The drama team and script
- [ ] A business person props
- [ ] Some pretend money

SUGGESTED SONGS
Be aware that visitors may not know the songs that you're singing and may not want to sing words that they don't yet understand or believe, so be sensitive in the songs that you choose. Try to include as many songs from **POLar EXPLOrers** as you can:
- 'God made you and me', *Light for Everyone* CD
- 'Anyone can come to God', *Reach Up!* CD
- 'You are good', *Follow You*, Hillsong Kids
- 'Trust and obey', *Follow You*, Hillsong Kids
- 'I will sing the wondrous story', *Songs of Fellowship* 278
- 'Tell out my soul', *Songs of Fellowship* 520
- 'Searching for your truth', the **POLar EXPLOrers** theme song
- 'Speedy shoes', the **POLar EXPLOrers** *Learn and remember* song

SERVICE 2 **programme**

Welcome
This style of service may offer a perfect opportunity to display some of the children's creativity from the club, if you have a suitable space. Make sure you have team members on the door to welcome the children and their families and show them where things are. If you can recreate some of your **POLar EXPLOrers** set in your worship space, that would be ideal. It might be helpful for your regular congregation if someone who usually leads the service does the welcome, but do try to include Sir Random Finds and Bare Feet in leading other parts.

Start with a well-known song or hymn. Follow this with your *Basic training* getting dressed race – ideally with adult participants who have not been part of the club. Have your leader board on stage to add in the new times.

Drama: *The Ice Adventure*
In this, the concluding part of the drama, everyone is working together

well as a team. They recap the lessons they learnt on their journey.

Set the scene
Create a PowerPoint presentation of different animal footprints (a PowerPoint is available to download on the **POLar EXPLOrers** website). Ask the congregation to guess which animals the prints belong to. Finish with a person's footprints. Say that you've been thinking about footprints during **POLar EXPLOrers**.

Invite Bare Feet to come and give everyone a definition of a carbon footprint: 'the amount of carbon dioxide released into the atmosphere as a result of the activities of a particular individual, organisation or community.' She can explain that that's what she's been trying to find out about on her expeditions, but instead what she's really discovered is something about a different footprint.

Ask the children to say what sort of footprint – a Kingdom Footprint. Say that we believe that Jesus is the King

of creation and that one day everyone will come to recognise him as the King and that the whole earth will be his kingdom. Until then, we know that because we have chosen to make Jesus our King, wherever we go, we can show his kingdom to other people. When we do the things he asks us to, we help to show his kingdom to the world around us, leaving good marks and changes on it – we call them Kingdom Footprints.

Ice-breaker
Sir Random Finds can introduce himself here and tell everyone how many famous explorers he's known in his time. He can say that during the club, we've thought about five key people (*or however many of the sessions you have done*) who went on God's big expedition with him, even though they seemed unlikely candidates. Remind everyone that God's big expedition is when Jesus' friends go out to help other people to start being friends of Jesus too. Have a PowerPoint or other method to display

the names of each of the characters you've looked at and the 'Never too…' phrase that went with each. Invite the children who've been at the club to offer as much information about the story of each character as they can. Do make sure that the PA is up to the job of making the children heard!

Finish by asking the children if they can remember the *Learn and remember* verse you've been using during the club. You could also sing the *Learn and remember* song, if you've been using it.

Bible reading

Remind everyone that the last character you looked at was Timothy and we learned that you are 'Never too young to be part of God's big expedition'. Timothy went on a big expedition with Paul and Silas and Luke, who wrote all the stories down. It would be good if you could project a map of Paul's second missionary journey at this point so that you can point out where today's story happens in the context of the rest of the trip.

Invite someone to read Acts 16:11–15. As it is so short, one of the children might like to read, although do give them some coaching on the difficult place names!

Talk

Ask the children who they think the character is in today's story. If no one responds with 'Lydia', read again Acts 16:13,14 and repeat the question. Remind everyone of the names of the characters you have met during the club, then ask what's different about this character. Hopefully they will notice that this is the only female. Say that this is interesting because in those days it was often men that got to do the exciting stuff. So being a woman makes her a little bit unlikely to be part of God's big expedition in that time and place. Invite a girl or woman (who has already been primed) to stand at the front and be a reminder point that Lydia was unlikely because she was a woman.

The Bible tells us that Lydia sold expensive purple cloth. She was a business woman. She was probably very busy but she made time to listen to Paul and his friends and she put her faith in Jesus. Sometimes we look at busy important people and think that they are unlikely to want to hear about Jesus and get involved in his big expedition. But Lydia really did get involved – she didn't just put her faith in Jesus, she invited Paul and his friends to come and stay with her. Give your female volunteer some business-like props (eg jacket, tie, briefcase, mobile phone) to remind everyone that Lydia seemed unlikely because she was busy and important.

The fact that Lydia sold purple cloth is really important to the story too; purple cloth was very valuable and worn by rich people – often royalty. Lydia would have probably been very wealthy. In the stories of Jesus, we often see that it is poor people that come to put their trust in him; there are stories about rich people not wanting to get involved because they think they have everything that they need. We might think that it's unlikely for a rich person to want to hear about Jesus, but Lydia did. And probably her being rich gave her resources to help in God's big expedition. Certainly it meant that she had space for unexpected visitors to stay with her. Give your volunteer a big wad of monopoly money or similar to remind people that Lydia seemed unlikely because she was wealthy.

Say that the last unlikely thing about Lydia's story is where it happened. Can anyone remember where Lydia talked to Paul? It was by the river, this would have been outside the city walls. Philippi was a foreign city and on its gates was a notice that said that people were forbidden to bring different religions into the city. It seemed unlikely that Paul, Silas, Timothy and Luke would be able to do any of God's big expedition in the city but they found a way, and at the river they met someone who, although unlikely, put her trust in Jesus.

The story doesn't stop with Lydia, though. The Bible tells us that her whole household were baptised (washed clean with water to show they wanted to start their lives afresh as friends of Jesus). That doesn't even mean just her family – a household in those days was a much bigger thing of extended family, household staff, people that were regularly connected with you through business. It could have been quite a lot of people, and because Lydia put her faith in Jesus, a whole community of people got to hear about him as well.

Ask the congregation to recap why Lydia was an unlikely person to be part of God's big expedition. Say that there are lots of reasons why we might think people are unlikely to want to know about Jesus: they are too busy, their lives seem to be perfect already, they might be part of another religion, they might have a very important job or celebrity lifestyle or we might never have gone anywhere near that subject with them because we are scared to. No one is too unlikely to be God's friend. Thank God too that we are 'Never too unlikely to be part of God's big expedition'.

Response

Ask people to reflect on why they or people they know seem unlikely people to be involved in God's big expedition. Pray, asking that God would speak to unlikely people to bring them into his kingdom and family. It might be that there is testimony of children and adults who have come to faith during the club that you could share here. Have people on hand who can talk to visitors who feel they are interested in finding out more about following Jesus.

Prayer

Pray that everyone who's been involved with the club would know that there is nothing that can stop them from being part of God's big expedition. Pray that they would know that they are making Kingdom Footprints as they go out into the world.

Be sure to flag up any future community events, special services, alpha courses etc. Make sure your team are focused on meeting the families of the children during refreshments after the service.

EXPEDITION STORE

EXPEDITION STORE 1
construction

Polar Explorer **constructions**

Construction 1
Life Size *Polar Explorer*

What you need
- Large rolls of white paper (wallpaper paper is perfect)
- Pens and pencils
- Scissors
- Fabric scraps
- Glitter
- Feathers
- Wool
- Paint
- Cardboard tubes (wrapping paper tubes are the sort of size)
- String
- Sticky tape/glue

What you do

If you have purchased rolls of paper, in preparation unroll the paper and roll it the other way so it is flat.

Form the children into groups of two or three and explain that each group is going to create their very own ***Polar Explorer***.

Ask one member of each group to lie down on the paper in an interesting/explorer position and draw around them. Cut around the outline.

Use paint to cover your ***Polar Explorer*** and use wool for hair.

While the paint is drying, use fabric scraps to make clothing and accessories for your ***Polar Explorer***. Use glitter, feathers (and any other decorative materials you may have) to add to your ***Polar Explorer***.

Give each group one cardboard tube to decorate. Show them how to thread string through the tube and tie at the top. Attach the ***Polar Explorer*** to the tube using sticky tape or glue.

Construction 2
Explorer map

What you need
- Sheets of thick white card (one per child) A4 or A3 – depending how big you want each child's map to be
- Old maps
- Waterproof markers
- Scissors
- Glue

What you do

Challenge the children to imagine that the town where they live has become a polar country.

Give each child a sheet of thick white card and invite them to use the markers to draw out the map. The children could try and think of different names to give familiar places in their town, for example:
- The Polar Park
- Snow-capped Cafe
- ***Polar Explorer*** School

Cut the old maps into small squares and, once they have put all their places on their map, encourage the children to use the squares of old maps to cover the rest of the map.

Construction 3
Woven compass
(to collect anything you find while out on a mission)

What you need
- Styrofoam soup bowls
- Brown acrylic paint
- Balls of string – brown or neutral colour
- Paint brushes
- Beads
- Scissors
- Sticky tape
- Craft knife (adult use only)
- Arrow shape from page 90 (can be pre-cut or the children can cut their own)
- Split pins
- Pens

What you do
Paint the bowl with brown acrylic paint (two coats may be needed) and cut seven slits on the side of the bowl. (Try to evenly mark out where the cuts will be.)

With the scissors, make evenly spaced cuts from the rim of the bowl all the way to the bottom. Take the ball of string and tie a knot at the end. (If you are short of time, these steps could be done in advance. For younger children, the next step could be started.)

Show the children how to place the string in one of the cuts and slide it down to the bottom so that the knot is on the inside and the rest of the ball is on the outside. Help them to start weaving, in and out, in and out. As they work their way around, encourage them to keep pushing the string down so that it all looks nice and even.

When they get near to the top, measure out enough string to go around another two and a half times, and then cut that length away from the ball of string. Take some tape and secure the end of the string so that it is easier to thread the beads on, then give each child some beads. Show them how to take two beads at a time and place them on the string, then weave through one slot. Encourage them to keep working all the way around adding the beads to the outside of the weaving.

Tie another knot at the end of the string, making it as close to the bowl as possible and so that it sits on the inside of the bowl. Tuck the knot in behind the string that runs on the inside.

Invite the children to turn their bowl upside down and mark out N E S W for north, east, south and west.

Have a helper or leader pierce a hole in the centre of the base of the bowl. Encourage the children to cut an arrow shape and use a split pin to secure it into the hole in the base of the bowl (for younger children, the split pin should be inserted by a helper or leader).

Construction 4
Explorer binoculars

What you need
- 1 kitchen roll cardboard tube per child
- Card (variety of colours)
- Decorative materials (stickers, pens, pencils, glitter etc)
- Paint
- Scissors
- PVA glue
- Sequins
- Sticky tape
- String

What you do
Cut the kitchen cardboard roll in half (this could be done beforehand in preparation) and give each child two halves. Invite them to paint both halves and then set them aside to dry.

Encourage each child to choose a piece of coloured card and decorate one side.

When the paint is dry, show the children how to place a line of glue down both long ends of the piece of decorated card. Encourage them to place the cardboard rolls down on the glue, and then let the glue dry.

Invite the children to use PVA glue to attach sequins around the binoculars, and then to add a strap by taping a piece of string onto their binoculars, so they can wear them around their neck.

Construction 5
Travel backpack

What you need
- Large shoeboxes (1 per child)
- Lots of white paper (A5 and A6) cut into rectangles
- Pictures of flags (optional)
- Pens and pencils
- Glue sticks
- Scissors
- Craft knife (adult use only)
- Florist ribbon

What you do
Ask each child to choose a shoebox for their backpack.

Give the children paper rectangles and invite them to draw pictures of polar countries (eg Canada, Norway). You could have the flags for them to copy.

Encourage the children to think of different countries, or words they associate with travelling, and to write these on more paper rectangles.

Invite the children to attach all their rectangles to their shoe box. Encourage them to point them in different directions, overlap the rectangles and make sure the whole box is covered.

To make the backpack straps, using a craft knife (adults only) to make a thin slit (the width of the ribbon) at each corner of the box (four slits in total). Invite each child to choose a colour of ribbon, and help them to thread the ribbon through the slits, tying them together to form two loops. Make sure the child can wear the straps.

Invite the children to glue the lid to the box and wear their backpack.

Bible **constructions**

Expedition 1
Flame headbands

What you need
- A strip of card 8 cm x 50 cm per child
- Decorative materials: pens, pencils, stickers, glitter
- Yellow, red and orange tissue paper
- PVA glue
- Glue spreaders
- Scissors
- Flame-shaped pieces of card (one per child); template on page 90
- Small pieces of card 1 cm x 4 cm
- Pens
- Staples and stapler or sticky tape

What you do
Give each child an 8 cm x 50 cm strip of card and invite them to decorate it with craft materials, for example pens, stickers or glitter. Then give each child a flame shape and encourage them to decorate it with red, orange and yellow tissue paper and then glue it to the middle of the headband.

Using smaller bits of paper (1 cm x 4 cm), ask the children if they know any words in other languages. Help them to write these words on the smaller bits of paper and glue them to the larger strip of card.

Wrap the band around the head of the child and staple or sticky tape it in place so that it can be easily slipped on and off (if you use staples, tape over them to prevent scratching).

Remind the children that during the story what looked like flames or tongues of fire appeared and settled on everyone. And they all were filled with the Holy Spirit and began speaking in other languages.

Expedition 2
Fruit pizzas

What you need
- 1/2 cup butter, soft
- 3/4 cup white sugar
- 1 egg
- 1 1/4 cups plain flour
- 1 teaspoon cream of tartar
- 1/2 teaspoon baking soda
- 1/4 teaspoon salt
- 1 package cream cheese
- 1/2 cup white sugar
- 2 teaspoons vanilla extract
- Variety of unusual fruits (if you can get an Ugli fruit this would be perfect to illustrate the story of Stephen – an unglamorous fruit but still does a brilliant job by tasting delicious)

Cooking equipment
- 2 large mixing bowls
- 2 spoons
- Pizza pan/large baking tray
- Large circular cutter (optional)
- Chopping board
- Knife (adult use only)

What you do
Preheat oven to 175º C (350º F).

As a group, cream together the butter and 3/4 cup sugar in a bowl until smooth. Mix in the egg. Combine the flour, cream of tartar, baking soda and salt; stir into the creamed mixture until just blended.

Press this dough into an ungreased pizza pan. (You could bake one large pizza or cut into individual pizzas using a circular cutter.)

Bake the pizza in a preheated oven for 8 to 10 minutes, or until lightly browned, and then allow to cool.

While the dough is cooking, in a large bowl, beat the cream cheese with 1/2 cup sugar and the vanilla extract until light. Spread this mixture on the cooled crust.

Cut up the fruit (adult only) and then encourage the children to use it to either decorate a slice of the large pizza or their own individual small pizza.

Expedition 3
Chariot craft

What you need

- Double yoghurt pots (one per child)
- Small squares of coloured paper
- PVA glue
- Glue spreaders
- Lollipop sticks (one per child)
- Squares of fabric
- Air-dry clay
- Clay modelling tools
- Thin strips of card (one per child)
- Horse body template (one per child)
- Googley eyes
- Brown wool
- Wooden clothes pegs (two per child)

What you do

Give each child a yoghurt pot and encourage them to use squares of coloured paper to cover it, creating a mosaic design.

Next, give each child a lollipop stick to turn into Philip. Show them how to use a square of fabric (roughly 10 cm x 10 cm) to wrap around the lollipop stick to create clothing. Help them to create a head for their lollipop stick by rolling a ball of air-dry clay. Encourage them to use clay modelling tools to carve facial features (mouth, eyes, nose, hair), then push the head securely onto the lollipop stick.

Give each child a horse body template to colour in, and two googley eyes to stick on each side of the template. Encourage them to use brown wool to create a tail and a mane for their horse, and to pin two clothes pegs to the bottom of the template to create legs.

Hand out thin strips of card (2 cm x 12 cm) and invite the children to stick the horse to one end and the chariot to the other end. Help them to add two circles to the sides of the yoghurt pot to create chariot wheels and then place their Philip lollipop person inside the yoghurt pot.

Expedition 4
Forgiveness stones

What you need

- Pebbles (1 per child)
- Paint in a variety of colours
- Paint brushes
- Glitter glues

What you do

Invite each child to choose a pebble and encourage them to paint their stone using the paints provided.

Once the paint has dried, help them to use glitter glues to write the word 'Forgiveness' on the pebble. You could use this opportunity to talk about how Stephen forgave the men who hurt him, and even asked God to forgive them.

Expedition 5
Life of Timothy comic strip

This activity is intended to be a whole group activity. The finished construction could be displayed around the team HQ.

What you need

- A3 paper
- Pens and pencils
- Bibles
- Black card (thin)

What you do

As a group, look at the story of Timothy and decide the important parts, eg:

- Timothy's grandma and mum teach him about the Bible
- Paul goes to Lystra where Timothy and his family live
- Paul wants Timothy to go on his journey with him
- Paul and Timothy go from town to town talking to people and helping the church
- Paul continues his travels with Silas
- Paul and Silas are sent to prison
- Paul writes to Timothy encouraging him to always be faithful and not be afraid of telling people about God

Split the group into pairs and give each pair one of the parts of Timothy's story. Give each pair a sheet of A3 paper and pens and pencils, and invite them to create one scene of the comic strip by illustrating their part of the story.

Once each pair has completed their part of the comic strip, construct a frame using black card to go around the outside of each A3 box. Put the images in order and stick them up around the room.

EXPEDITION STORE 2
Games

X marks the spot

What you need

- A large world map (A1 or A2 size) with a small polar explorer figure drawn on it
- Small sticky notes with an 'X' drawn on (one per child)
- Pens
- Blindfolds

What you do

Stick the map onto a wall.

Give each child an X sticky note and ask them to write their name on it.

Blindfold the children one at a time and spin them around three or four times. Encourage them to try to stick their X on the polar explorer on the map.

The child that places their X closest to the polar explorer wins.

East West
(a variation of the game Port Starboard)

What you need

- A large space
- A helper or leader to call out instructions
- List of instructions from page 91

What you do

Invite the children to find a space. Read out the list of instructions and the action for each one – go through these twice to help the children to remember them.

Challenge the children to listen as you read the instructions in random order. After a few practice turns, the children who do the wrong action or who are slowest to complete the action are out.

Pass the backpack

What you need

- A large chocolate bar
- Lots of different sized bags, plus a backpack
- Pieces of paper or sticky labels with commands written on them
- Music

What you do

In advance, place a chocolate bar in a small paper bag. Write a command on the outside of the bag, such as, 'Dance a jig', then place that bag inside another bag, on which another silly command is written (command ideas on page 92). Continue placing bags inside of bags (all with silly commands on them) until you have at least one for each player. (Ideas for commands are available to download from the **POLaR EXPLORErS** website.) Place the collection of bags inside your backpack.

Tell the children that, in order to retrieve the chocolate, they must complete the backpack game.

Invite everyone to sit in a circle and begin passing the backpack as you play music. When you stop the music, the player holding the bag must open the first bag, stand up and perform the task. After each task is successfully completed, encourage the whole group to give that person a round of applause.

Continue playing in this manner until everyone has performed a command and the bag containing the chocolate is revealed. To celebrate successfully completing all the tasks, share out the chocolate.

Note: if the children do not feel confident to complete the tasks, encourage helpers and leaders to help them.

Polar pairs

What you need

- The following words and matching pictures (or two copies of each word) on individual A4 sheets of paper (available to download from the **POLar EXPLOrers** website), enough copies for one sheet per child: flag, torch, compass, tent, map, walking boots, binoculars, first aid kit, magnifying glass, rope, camera
- Music

What you do

Place all the words and pictures, face down, on the floor.

Tell the children that they need to sort out what to take on their exploring mission. All the things they need are on the sheets of paper, but it's their mission to match them up.

Play music and encourage the children to dance or move around. When the music stops, invite them to stand on a sheet of paper. When everyone is on a sheet, invite the children to pick up their sheet (give a signal for this) and find their pair (match up the words and pictures).

If you want to make it competitive, the last pair to join up could be out.

Invite the children to place their sheet of paper face down and back on the floor, mix them up a bit, and repeat.

Sleeping bag race

What you need

- Sleeping bags (one per team)
- Cones to mark out the start and finish
- A whistle

What you do

Divide the children into teams of up to five.

Give each team a sleeping bag and explain that, on the whistle, the children must take it in turns to get into the sleeping bag and jump to the end of the course and back. When they get back, they must get out of the sleeping bag and tag the next person in the team, who then gets into the sleeping bag and repeats the process.

When everyone in the team has been to the end of the course and back in the sleeping bag, they must sit down. The quickest team (the one to sit down first) is the winner.

Scavenger hunt

What you need

- A copy of the scavenger hunt checklist for each team (page 93)
- A pen or pencil per team
- A bag for every team
- A leader or helper for each team
- Prizes (optional)

What you do

Before the children arrive, make sure the items on the list are hidden. You could hide enough for all groups to find one of each item or just hide one or two of each.

Divide the children into groups of four and assign an adult to monitor each group during their hunt. Give each group a copy of the scavenger hunt checklist (page 93), a pencil or pen and a bag.

Send the groups to start searching for the items on their list, and instruct them to place all the items they find in their bag.

Once a team finds all the items, they must hurry back to you for you to check their bag. The first team to come back with all the items wins (a prize, if you are giving one).

Ten Pin Poling

What you need

- 20 empty bottles (fizzy drinks bottles work well for this)
- Two tennis balls painted white – to represent snowballs
- Cones

What you do

Set out the empty bottles in two ten-pin formations, and set up a cone about 8 m away from the pins.

Divide the children into two teams, North and South, and number the children in each team. Give each team a 'snowball'.

Call out one number at a time. Challenge the child in each team who has been assigned that number to run to the cones and roll their snowball' to knock down as many of their pins as possible. Ask a helper to keep the score and to reset the pins each time they are knocked down. (Deduct a point for each of the opposition's pins they knock down.)

When everyone has had at least one turn, or you've run out of time, add up the scores and declare a winning team.

Island relay

What you need
- Two large sheets of card, preferable A0, per team
- Two medium sheets of card, approximately A1, per team
- Two small sheets of card, approximately A2, per team
- Cones to mark out the start and finish
- A large space

What you do
Separate children into teams of 8 to 10, and appoint one member of the team as captain. Give each team two large sized sheets of card.

Explain that the captain must get their whole team from one end of the space to the other end of the space (marked out by cones), but they can only travel using the sheets of card. The captains must get their whole team onto one sheet of card (including themselves), then place the second sheet of large card in front and transfer everyone across. They must repeat this until everyone has travelled across to the other end of the space.

Once the captain has successfully got their team to the end of the space, challenge them to go back using the two medium sheets of card. This time the captains may have to make more than one trip if their whole team doesn't fit on the card.

Then repeat with the small sheet of card.

The first team to successfully travel to the end of the space on the small card is the winning team

What's in the backpack?

What you need
- A backpack
- Various items to be put in the backpack, such as: keys, a frisbee, a spoon, gloves, a whistle, a notepad, a magnifying glass, a tambourine, a clothes peg
- A sheet of paper and pen/pencil per team
- A chair
- A whistle

What you do
Divide the children into two teams and invite the teams to line up at one end of the room. Place the backpack (complete with contents) on a chair at the other end of the room (supervised by a leader or helper). Tell the teams how many different objects there are in the backpack.

On the whistle, challenge team members to run (or jump, skip, hop – leaders could decide the action) to the backpack in turn, one at a time. Invite each child to reach into the backpack and feel around for an object and try to work out what it is. The leader or helper supervising the backpack must make sure children don't look inside.

Once they think they have identified an object, the child must run back to their team and write it down on the sheet of paper. Then the next member of the team must run and identify another object.

When each team has written down the correct number of objects, take out each object in turn and invite the teams to tick it off their list if they identified it correctly. The team with the most correct objects is the winner.

Variation: if children are younger, then the person supervising the backpack could add one item to the bag at the time (to make it easier for children to feel and identify).

Globe grabbers

What you need
- Lots of balloons blown up
- Badminton net and posts
- A large space
- Whistle
- A stopwatch

What you do
Place the badminton net in the middle of the space. Divide the children into two teams and put the teams on opposite sides of the net. Split the balloons equally between the two teams.

Explain to the teams that when you blow the whistle they have one minute to throw as many 'globes' as possible (the balloons) over into the opposing team's side. At the end of the minute the winning team is the team that has the least number of 'globes' on their side.

RULES:
- Each child can only hold one 'globe' at a time.
- The children must throw the 'globes' over the net (any globes thrown under the net should be put back on their original side – you need to have helpers assigned to this task).
- If a 'globe' is popped, it is added to the total of whichever team popped it.

EXPEDITION STORE 3
Drama SCRIPTS
The Ice Adventure

The Ice Adventure is the story of four adventurers battling through the polar wastes with a vital message for the scientist Yvonne Von Evian, stationed beyond the snow plains, across the glacier and around the mountain.

Characters

- **Great Scott** – the elder statesman of the group. Old-fashioned, experienced and wearer of a fine moustache. But, he is an imposter!

- **Fay Mears** – the outdoor survival specialist. She has spent many a happy day marooned in the middle of nowhere.

- **Helen 'Helter' Skelter** – the woman of action. She can ski, snowboard, drive huskies, ride a snowmobile… often at the same time.

- **Prince Larry** – a member of the royal family. The others see him as a bit of liability.

- **Chief** – head of **POLar EXPLOrers**, only ever heard over the radio.

- **Yvonne Von Evian** – the scientist the group is trying to reach. She only appears in the final episode, and is about 18 or 20 years old.

- **Some non-speaking servants of Prince Larry**.

Service 1

If you don't use this episode in a service, put it early in your programme for the first day of the club.

Scene

Base camp. The stage is empty apart from some radio equipment to one side. The characters enter, bringing with them all sorts of equipment: skis, boxes, backpacks, huge coats etc, apart from Larry, who is only carrying a shoebox. As they stagger in, they collide with each other, dropping things, getting tangled up and generally causing havoc.

Fay: (*Still trying to hold onto her equipment while avoiding the others.*) Wait a minute, wait a minute! We're not getting anywhere. Everyone put whatever they're carrying down!

The four of them drop everything with an almighty crash.

Larry: Ooh, I feel like my arms are going to fall off!

Helen: What? Why? You were barely carrying anything!

Larry: These arms aren't used to carting things about. There's not much call for that when you're a Prince. Usually, I have a servant or five to do it for me.

Fay: (*Looking at Larry with dislike.*) I don't know why **POLar EXPLOrers** allowed you to come – you've never done anything more dangerous than eat a yogurt that was a day past its sell-by date.

Scott: Nonsense! I'm sure His Royal Highness Prince Laurence of the North Seas, the vast and endless Highlands, the awesome Great Plains and Croydon town centre will be fine. We all have to start somewhere. I remember when I first started out, I can't have been more than 16 or 17. I joined a team racing to the summit of Mount…

Fay: (*Cutting him off, before he gets going on his story.*) OK, OK! I get the picture. We'll give him the benefit of the doubt. (*She looks at the congregation and realises that there's an audience.*) Oh! Hello everyone. Are you here for the expedition briefing too? Well, we'd better introduce ourselves. I'm Fay Mears, survival expert extraordinaire. (*She strikes a heroic pose.*)

Helen: (*Pushing past Fay and striking an even more heroic pose.*) Helen 'Helter' Skelter's the name, action's the game. If you can jump off it, ski down it or skate across it, I've done it!

Scott: (*Walking forward, twirling his moustache.*) I'm Scott – Great Scott they call me, because of all the polar adventures I've had over the years – Canada, southern Argentina, Norway, Siberia, Antarctica, Alaska…

Helen: (*Sniggering.*) The frozen food section of the supermarket…

Scott: What?

Helen: Nothing!

Larry: (*Apologetically coming forward.*) I'm Prince Larry, here because… well I'm actually not sure why I'm here. I've never really done anything like this before.

Fay: (*Looking at him unhappily.*) Yes. Quite. Anyway, we're waiting for our instructions. Are you coming to **POLar EXPLorers** this week? I'm sure my friends Sir Random Finds and Bare Feet will look after you well – they're great explorers!

The radio starts cracking. They all rush over to it.

Chief: (*Speaking through an off-stage mic.*) Come in base camp. Hello base camp, this is HQ calling.

Fay: (*Picking up the mouthpiece for the radio and speaking into it.*) This is base camp, hello Chief. How are you?

Chief: Ooh, not very well. My frostbite is still playing up. I should never have gone out in that blizzard just wearing flip-flops.

Everyone winces and Larry clutches his toes.

Fay: We're all here and ready, Chief, where are we going?

Chief: We're sending you with a vital message to Professor Yvonne Von Evian, the scientist based at Ice Station Debra. She's been cut off for months and all her communications are down.

Helen: Cool! I've always wanted to meet Prof Yvonne Von Evian!

Larry: Sounds a bit dangerous.

Scott: Don't worry! It'll be a piece of cake – all we have to do is trek across the snow plains, scale a glacier, climb a mountain and we'll be there!

Larry: Can I not just eat the cake? (*He looks carefully at Scott.*) Hang on, are you wearing a false moustache?

Scott: (*Covering his top lip.*) What? No! Of course not! What a silly suggestion.

Fay: Sssshhh! (*Speaking into the mouthpiece.*) What's the message, Chief?

Chief: I can't tell you over the radio, you'll receive a coded message very soon! That's all from me, HQ out!

Fay: Bye Chief! (*She puts the mouthpiece back.*) Right team, we've got a lot to prepare for. (*Everyone starts to pick up their stuff and makes to leave.*) We've got to take a message out into the wilderness! See you at **POLar EXPLorers** everyone!

Helen: Excellent!

Scott: Jolly good!

Larry: Oh dear…

• •

Episode 1

Scene

Base camp – the place is strewn with equipment and winter clothing. The radio is in the corner. Great Scott enters, wearing a coat, scarf, old-fashioned hat and carrying some wooden tennis rackets.

Scott: (*To himself.*) Well, so far so good. I've managed to fool the others into thinking I'm Great Scott, the legendary explorer! Well, I'm not! The Chief turned me down for a place on his team and so I'm going to ruin this expedition. That will teach him to ignore me! (*He starts laughing, but stops abruptly when Fay and Helen enter.*) Er, hello! I think I've got everything I need. How about you two?

Fay: Where is it?

Scott: What?

Helen: Your stuff!

Scott: I'm wearing it!

Fay and Helen: What?

Fay: You can't just take that, it's -30°C at the pole!

Helen: Where are your waterproofs, windproofs, snow-proofs, polar-bear proofs?

Scott: Ha! I don't need those! When I scaled the north face of Kilimanjaro, all I needed was a tweed jacket, a pair of slippers and a big bag of liquorice allsorts.

Fay: Seriously, you need more than that. We've got to stay safe, and keep each other safe. If we let you go out in the cold in those clothes, you'll freeze solid and we'll be able to use you as a table!

Scott: Well, I suppose an extra coat wouldn't hurt. (*Fay helps him put on a big waterproof coat.*) Mm, it's quite nice.

Larry enters, wearing a bright shirt, shorts and flippers.

Larry: Hello chaps! I'm ready to go!

Helen: Oh not you as well!

Larry: Only kidding. I've got lots of warm stuff. (*Shouting off-stage.*) Bring it in!

Some servants appear, carrying boxes and boxes of stuff. Include as much ludicrous and unwieldy stuff – skis, snowboard, climbing ropes, tents – as you can.

Fay: Where did all this come from?

Larry: I just got my dad to order everything for me. I thought, if we're going to take a message to an important scientist across snowfields, over glaciers and up and down mountains, I'd better be prepared. And best of all, I got this massive cake! (*He opens a box, takes out a cake and starts munching it.*)

Helen: Well, all this is brilliant! I can do lots of daredevil stuff with this. (*She picks out bits of equipment and mimes everything as she describes it.*) Climb walls of ice, ride through icy forests, ski down mountains, fight off polar bears… I'll be famous after this!

Fay: But you are famous, aren't you? I thought I'd heard of you, so I looked you up on the internet. (*She pulls out a sheet of paper.*) Ah yes, that was it. You were the navigator of that expedition that got lost on the way to Lapland, weren't you?

Helen: Erm, yeah, sort of.

Scott: How did you get lost?

Helen: I missed the right track because I was making a skiing video for my YouTube channel.

Fay: And you were on the team that went to northern Canada and got stuck in the ice.

Helen: Er…

Larry: What did you get wrong that time?

Helen: Well, when I was ordering the supplies, I ticked the wrong box on the form and instead of a large Arctic ship, I ended up with a large bag of chips. Anyone could have made the same mistake!

Fay: What about the adventure to the Antarctic where you got attacked by penguins?

Helen: Well, how was I to know that penguins love to eat the hi-energy biscuits we had?

Fay: You kept dropping them on the floor.

Helen: Well, I was scared of losing our way, so I thought I'd leave a trail of crumbs – you know, like Hansel and Gretel!

Fay: I don't believe it. I've got an old explorer who thinks he can go anywhere as long as he's got an old tennis racquet and a bag of toffees, a Prince who can't go anywhere without his servants and now someone who has made

so many mistakes, I'm surprised she hasn't been on *You've Been Framed!* There's no way we can go on this expedition. I'm calling HQ. (*She goes over to the radio and picks up the mouthpiece.*) Hello HQ, this is base camp. Come in HQ.

We hear the voice of the Chief over the radio.

Chief: Hello base camp. What's the problem?

Fay: It's the team you put together, Chief, I'm afraid they're not up to the job!

Larry: Hang on a minute!

Scott: That's not fair!

Helen: (*Glumly.*) She's right.

Fay: One's too old, one's too inexperienced and Helen Skelter can't seem to do anything right. She's made so many mistakes, I'm surprised she's still alive!

Chief: Fay, Fay. Let me stop you there. HQ knows all about Helen's past mistakes. But we know she's learnt her lesson and we selected her especially for this mission.

During the conversation, Helen gets more and more happy.

Fay: What? Really?

Chief: Yes, Fay. Each one of you has been chosen to play your part, including Helen. She's a brave woman, who has just got it wrong in the past. We think all she needs is some encouragement, a new compass and a lesson on the difference between ships and chips.

Fay: But…

Chief: No 'buts' Fay. You're all on this expedition together. If you work together, you'll be fine and we can get the message to Professor Yvonne Von Evian safely. HQ out. (*The radio goes silent.*)

Fay: (*Putting the mouthpiece down in disbelief.*) Well, I suppose we're all on the team, no matter how crazy, unprepared or accident-prone we are…

Helen: Amazing! (*She hugs Fay.*)

Larry: Excellent!

Scott: (*Aside.*) And I can blame Helen when everything goes wrong.

Fay: What?

Scott: Er… Um… I said, I'm so happy I could burst into song! (*He launches into an awkward rendition of 'The Happy Wanderer' or 'Climb Every Mountain'. The others look at him as if he's crazy.*)

Larry: Are you sure you're not wearing a fake moustache?

Scott: (*Getting out his hankie to cover his mouth.*) Of course not! (*He sneezes unconvincingly.*)

Fay: Well, let's get all this stuff packed up. We need to get going!

Fay, Helen and Scott start to gather everything up, but they keep dropping things. Larry watches for a few seconds, then turn to shout off-stage.

Larry: I say, my good fellows, can you give me a hand?

Larry's servants come on, pick everything up and carry it off.

Helen: Well, I suppose being a prince does have its benefits, come on! Let's go on our expedition!

They all leave.

· ·

Episode 2

Scene
A hastily made encampment. Tents are half put-up, rucksacks and skis discarded haphazardly. Helen and Larry enter, carrying odd tent poles, pegs and a mallet. They are wearing all their cold weather gear, with scarves round their faces. For about 15 seconds, they gesticulate wildly at each other while making muffled noises, as if their scarves are distorting their speech. Eventually, Helen mimes that they should take their scarves off.

Helen: I thought you knew how to put up a tent!

Larry: I do! I give the tent and the instructions to the servants and they do it for me.

Helen: (*Groaning.*) Oh! You're in the middle of a frozen wasteland. You don't have any servants here.

Larry: (*Looking around.*) Oh. Yes.

Fay enters, carrying a snow shovel over her shoulder.

Fay: What are you two arguing about? (*She sees the tents and stops in her tracks.*) What are those? We can't sleep in those!

Helen: His Royal Highness here doesn't seem to know how to do anything without his servants.

Larry: Well, what about you? I thought you were an outdoor daredevil! You must have put a tent up before.

Helen: Er… Not this… Um… Not this kind…

Fay: I don't believe it.

As she says this, she turns away and forces Larry to duck to avoid being hit in the face with the snow shovel. During the next few lines, Fay should turn and move around the stage, causing both Helen and Larry to duck to avoid the shovel.

Larry: Look out!

Fay: (*Turning back.*) What? Is it a polar bear?

Helen: Watch what you're doing!

Fay: What I'm doing? Look at these tents! We can only get in them if we lie down flat!

Larry: Argh! You almost hit me in the face!

Fay: What do you mean? I will hit you in the face, if you don't get these tents sorted. Now where's Scott?

Scott enters, looking very bedraggled. He limps on, but gives an overly theatrical wink to the children. He's been up to no good.

Fay: Great Scott! Where have you been? What's happened to you?

She turns with one last swing of the snow shovel. This one knocks Larry over.

Larry: (*Getting up and rubbing his head.*) Put that shovel down!

Fay: Oh! Sorry!

She puts the shovel down and helps Larry upright, rubbing his head. Scott stands up straight, looking bored, waiting for someone to notice him.

Fay: What happened to you?

Scott: (*Forgetting he's meant to be injured.*) What do you mean? (*He realises his mistake and starts to hobble and groan again.*) Aaaaaah! Ow! Ow!

Helen: (*Rushing over to him.*) What's wrong?

Scott: Oh dear! Oh dear! I was trying to sort out the food, making sure we had enough for each day, when I was attacked by a giant white creature!

Larry: (*Shrieking.*) The abominable snowman! (*He leaps into Fay's arms.*)

Fay: (*Dropping him.*) Get off me! There's no such thing as the abominable snowman!

Scott: It was a giant polar bear. He must have been waiting for us! As soon as I unloaded some of the food, he was on top of me, trying to get all our supplies!

Helen: Eek!

Larry: Oh no!

Fay: It must have been a quiet polar bear, they usually roar really loudly! I never heard anything.

Scott: Er… yes… it was… (*He pauses to think.*) He… he was on a sponsored silence!

Larry: Oh, I've done one of those. I wasn't allowed to speak for a whole day! I did very well, I made it nearly to breakfast time!

Helen: (*Incredulous.*) A polar bear doing a sponsored silence?

Scott: (*Realising that didn't sound very convincing.*) Er, yes. (*Trying to change the subject.*) Anyway, he took all the food and ran off into the snow!

Fay: So, what's left?

Scott: Nothing.

Helen: Nothing?

Scott: Nothing.

Fay: What are we going to eat?

Helen: We're miles and miles from anywhere!

Larry: Not even a supermarket or a chip shop?

Fay: No!

Scott: I tried to fight him off, but he was too strong.

Helen: What are we going to do?

Fay: We'd better go and find out what we've got left! (*She, Helen and Larry run off.*)

Scott: (*Laughing.*) Well, that's ruined that! I threw almost all of the food off a cliff! I've saved enough for me, but not for them… (*The leaders should encourage the children to boo.*) Oh shut up! (*He laughs again, this time so much that his moustache starts to fall off – Scott can pull it away slightly with his hand while he laughs.*)

Fay: (*Coming back on with the others, shocked.*) There's nothing left.

Helen: Not a sausage.

Larry: Oh don't say sausages, I want one and I can't have one now. (*Looking at Scott.*) Great Scott! What's happened to your moustache?

Scott: (*Hurriedly sticking it back on his face.*) Oh, er, it must have frozen and the wind blew it off!

Fay: Well, unless we can hunt or fish some food, or find some plants, then we're done for.

Helen: The ice is too thick and I haven't seen a plant for miles!

Fay: (*Sitting down on a rucksack, dejectedly.*) That's it then. We're doomed.

Larry: Well, it's my birthday next week, and my mum didn't want me to miss out on my usual birthday feast, so she packed a small food parcel. (*He rummages in one of the bags.*) Here we go. (*He pulls out sandwiches wrapped in tin foil and passes them round.*)

Fay: Well, I suppose this will keep us going for a little while – we might be able to send a message. But the radio's been out since this morning. I think it must be the weather.

Larry: I think there's more stuff in the food parcel. Let me look. (*He looks back in the bag and calls the following list out over his shoulder.*) Yep, there's 24 freeze-dried chicken dinners, 16 freeze-dried lamb dinners, 10 freeze-dried fish and chips, 4 freeze-dried black forest gateaus, 8 tubs of ice cream and a Curly Wurly. Two Curly Wurlys. No wait a minute, there are ten! (*He turns back round holding a handful of Curly Wurlys.*)

Helen: How big are your birthday banquets?

Fay: Never mind that, how did you manage to carry all of that stuff? I've never seen you carrying anything heavier than a bacon double cheeseburger!

Larry: Oh, my mum's really good at packing bags. Shall we put the stove on and un-freeze-dry some chicken dinners?

Helen and Fay: Yes!

Larry picks up the food bag and he, Fay and Helen go off-stage. Scott is left alone – he is angry.

Scott: I don't believe it! How could that fool Larry suddenly have so much food! I'll have to think of something else to ruin this expedition!

There is a sound effect of a large crack and rumble. Scott starts to stagger and almost loses his balance.

Scott: Whoa! The ice, it's breaking up! The camp's not going to be safe for much longer. (*He steadies himself and has an idea.*) That's it! If we leave all the equipment here, it will either fall down a crack or just float away on the ice! And I can blame that idiot Helen and Prince Useless for pitching camp in the wrong place! (*He shouts off-stage.*) Wait for me!

He runs off. The children boo and hiss!

● ●

Episode 3

Scene

The stage is empty apart from snow. The team wearily trudge on. They have virtually no equipment: Larry is carrying his food bag, Fay has the radio on her back and Helen has a pair of skis over her shoulder.

Fay: Larry, your birthday banquet food parcel was a miracle, but we need another miracle now. All our equipment is gone!

Helen: (*To Scott.*) You were the last one in the camp, didn't you notice that anything was wrong?

Scott: No, not at all! I would have noticed if the ice was breaking up! (*He gets more and more animated as he tells the story. The others watch in disbelief.*) When I was in the Canadian Arctic in the 1960s, I got trapped on an ice floe in Payne Bay. Killer whales were circling all around and all I had to fight them off with was a box of toffee and some frozen baguettes. They leapt in the air, their jaws open wide, ready to eat me. As quick as a flash, I jammed their mouths open with the baguettes and threw the toffee in. They had to bite down so hard to snap the baguettes that their teeth got stuck together on the toffee! And I was rescued by the local missionary, driving a massive tractor.

Helen: A baguette?

Fay: A box of toffee?

Larry: A missionary on a massive tractor?

Helen: What rubbish!

Fay: You're making it up!

Larry: You're definitely wearing a false moustache…

Scott: (*Covering his mouth.*) No I'm not! Anyway, what I mean is I didn't notice anything was wrong when I joined you for our amazing freeze-dried chicken dinner.

Fay: I can't believe all our tents, our bags, skis… everything fell down that big crack in the ice.

Scott: Crevasse.

Larry: Well, there's no need to be rude!

Scott: No, my good fellow. A crack in the ice is called a crevasse.

Helen: What are we going to do? All we have is Larry's food, these skis and the radio, which I managed to rescue before it fell into the crevasse.

Fay: And the radio hasn't worked for ages. I don't know what's wrong with it.

Scott: Have you tried turning it off and turning it back on again?

Fay: Yes.

Helen: Have you tried changing the channels so you can try different frequencies?

Fay: Yes!

Larry: Have you tried tuning it in to Radio 2? I love listening to Chris Evans in the morning! (*He goes to fiddle with the radio.*)

Fay: (*Getting more and more annoyed.*) No, of course not! I've tried everything I can think of. Nothing works – it's broken or frozen or we're out of range or whatever. It's no use (*She shouts.*) IT DOESN'T WORK!

Suddenly the radio crackles into life. We hear the Chief's voice.

Chief: Hello Fay, come in Fay Mears, over.

Fay: Wh-what? (*To Larry.*) What happened? What did you do?

Larry: Er, I turned the volume up.

Fay: (*Picking up the mouthpiece.*) Chief! Chief! It's so good to hear your voice! We've lost all our equipment – the ice sheet broke up and it fell into a crevasse!

Chief: Don't worry Fay. We're checking your GPS location as we speak. We'll see whether anything is in range.

Larry: We're in the middle of nowhere. Nothing's going to be in range.

Helen: (*Sarcastically.*) Maybe there's a missionary on a tractor nearby.

Chief: We've checked our maps and computer records. It seems there's something 25 miles to the east of you. We're not quite sure what it is, because it was left there by a Swedish team quite a few years ago now. We're trying to contact the Swedish team to find out, but you could go and take a look.

Fay: We can't go 25 miles in this weather, it would take us over a day! We'd never survive without tents and the rest of our cold-weather gear!

Chief: Fay, it's the only option – there's nothing else around. You've got to go.

Helen: I'll go! I'm Helen 'Helter' Skelter! I can ski all the way there – it'll take much less time than walking.

Scott: Nonsense. You'll get lost – remember all the mistakes you made before?

Helen: If the Chief thinks I can be part of his expedition team, then you should too. And I've learnt from my mistakes! Anyway, we've got no choice but to try. You start walking east, and I'll ski on ahead and find out what's there!

Fay: She's right – you ski, Helen, we'll follow on. Come on guys.

Helen rushes off with the skis. The others walk in a circle around the stage a couple of times. As they go round, someone could throw fake snow over them. A sign saying 'Two hours later' is held up (or the words could appear on the screen). The radio crackles into life again, but this time, we hear Helen's voice.

Helen: Hello Fay, come in Fay. This is Helen, over.

Fay: (*Speaking into the mouthpiece.*) Helen! Wow! Are you there?

Helen: Of course – I'm Helter Skelter! And you won't believe what's here! It's a store full of stuff – food, equipment, tents and clothing! It's amazing! Chief was right to send us here!

Larry: Fantastic! (*He goes to high-five Scott, but Scott just looks at him, annoyed.*)

Scott: (*Bitterly.*) Yes. Brilliant.

Helen: I'll put some stuff onto a sledge and ski back to you, then we can all ski back to the Swedish store. They've even got meatballs!

Fay: I never thought we'd find the store – I thought 25 miles was just too far!

Larry: Let's have a Curly Wurly to celebrate! (*He takes three out of his bag and hands them round.*)

Fay: Thanks! Come on, let's go, the quicker we walk, the sooner we'll meet up with Helen. And the sooner we can get the Chief's message to Professor Yvonne Von Evian!

Fay and Larry run off. Scott stays on stage – he is fuming.

Scott: (*Throwing his Curly Wurly on the floor in disgust.*) I don't believe it! Everything I try to do to ruin this mission just doesn't work! This expedition should have failed by now and the Chief should have been disgraced. I'm still not giving up. This team is so stupid that another chance is bound to come up. Then the Chief will be sorry for turning me down.

He stomps off to the boos and hisses of the children and leaders.

Episode 4

Scene

Out in the snow, on the trail to find the Professor. There is snow and some fake rocks on stage. The team enter with lots of new equipment (this can be the original equipment, with Swedish flags stuck on it!) and all but Scott are wearing snow goggles. They are in good spirits, apart from Scott, who comes on last and is still angry. The weather is bad – occasionally, fake snow is thrown from the side of the stage.

Fay: That Swedish store was amazing! So much stuff!

Helen: Yeah, some great new skis and a snowboard!

Larry: (*Patting his stomach.*) And so many meatballs! I couldn't eat another thing!

Fay: It's a good job they had these snow goggles, the sun reflecting off the snow was really bright!

Helen: Where has the sun gone now? I can't believe it's snowing after such a clear blue sky.

Fay: The weather can change really quickly out here, you've got to be ready for anything.

Larry: After all those meatballs, I'm ready for a nap!

Helen: Well, maybe we could stop for a moment. We've been going for a few hours now, and it's getting more and more difficult.

They take off their packs and goggles and stretch or sit down on the fake rocks.

Fay: Well, I'm glad that this expedition is finally going according to plan. After losing all our food to a polar bear, and then all our equipment down a crevasse, I thought we were done for.

Helen: Yep, it's certainly been dangerous, but I'm Helen 'Helter' Skelter! I laugh in the face of danger! (*She laughs loudly in Larry's face.*)

Larry: Get off me! How are you doing Scott? You've not said much since we left the Swedish store.

Scott: (*Sulking.*) Humph. I'm fine. (*He starts blinking his eyes.*)

Helen: Are you OK?

Scott: Yes, I'm fine. The snow keeps getting in my eyes.

Some more fake snow is thrown on stage. It goes right in Scott's face.

Larry: Time for a snack? (*He pulls four Curly Wurlys out of his bag and hands them round.*)

Fay: You know, I'm going to send a big thank-you card to your mum when we get back. What a birthday banquet – it saved our lives!

Scott starts rubbing his eyes and moaning a bit.

Helen: Are you sure you're OK? What's wrong with your eyes?

Scott: (*Annoyed.*) There's nothing wrong with my eyes! Leave me alone you stupid woman!

Fay: (*Slightly taken aback.*) Alright, Scott. Keep it calm.

Suddenly Scott puts his hands over his eyes in pain, he crumples onto the floor. The others rush to kneel beside him.

Larry: Scott, what's wrong?

Helen: Are you OK?

Scott: My eyes! They hurt so much!

Fay: Scott, did you have your snow goggles on earlier?

Scott: No.

Larry: (*To Fay.*) Why, what difference would that make?

Fay: He's probably got photokeratitis.

Larry: Photo-who?

Helen: Kera-what?

Fay: Snow blindness. The bright sun reflecting off the snow earlier would have hurt his eyes badly. It's like sunburn, but in your eyes!

Larry: Ouch!

Fay: Quick, we need to get snow goggles on him.

Larry struggles with trying to put snow goggles on Scott. Finally he succeeds, but pulls Scott's fake moustache off at the same time.

Larry: (*Holding the moustache.*) Argh! (*He throws it at Helen, who screams.*)

Helen: (*Brushing the fake moustache off her and onto the floor.*) Eek! What is that?

Fay: (*Picking it up and looking at it.*) It's a fake moustache!

Larry: I knew it!

The radio crackles into life. We hear the Chief's voice.

Chief: HQ to Paul McSmall. Come in Paul McSmall.

Scott: What? Impossible! How do you know?

Helen: What? Who's Paul McSmall?

Fay: (*Speaking into the mouthpiece.*) Er, Chief, Fay here. Is that message meant for us? There's no one called Paul here.

Chief: Yes Fay. We've discovered that Great Scott isn't who he says he is. He is in fact Paul McSmall, an explorer who I turned down for a place at **POLar EXPLorers**.

Helen: (*Shocked.*) So you're not Great Scott!

Fay: (*Angry.*) You're an imposter!

Larry: (*Upset.*) And I shared my birthday banquet with you!

Scott/Paul: Chief? Is that you? How did you know?

Chief: Because the real Great Scott is sitting here, drinking hot chocolate with me.

Fay: But why?

Chief: We're not sure why, but another of our expedition teams found all your food at the bottom of a cliff, and when you told us that you'd lost your equipment too, we began to get suspicious.

Helen: (*To Scott/Paul.*) You threw our food off a cliff?

Larry: What? You mean you didn't get attacked by a polar bear doing a sponsored silence?

Chief: Why did you do it, Paul?

Scott/Paul: (*Less angry, more whining.*) You wouldn't take me on your expedition. You turned me down flat, without giving me a chance.

Chief: But that's not true, is it Paul? We would have given you a place, but you were too proud and mean to work with others – you wanted all the glory for yourself. If we'd given you a place, you could have put all your team in danger. And you have done that – Fay, Larry and Helen could have been killed.

Scott/Paul: (*Pausing before speaking.*) Yes. I suppose you're right. (*Quietly.*) I've even blinded myself because I was too proud to listen to Fay's advice about wearing snow goggles. Now I might never see again.

Chief: Yes, you will. You'll be better in a day or so, Fay should know what to do to help you get better. Paul, you're out there in the frozen wilderness and if you don't change your ways, you could die. You need to work with the others to get the message to the Professor. Can you do that, Paul?

Scott/Paul: Yes. I can.

Chief: Paul, you're going to have to rely on the others until you get better. Look after him, Fay. I have a feeling he may have learnt his lesson.

Fay: Will do, Chief. Fay Mears out. (*She puts down the mouthpiece.*) Come on guys, let's make camp over there. (*She points off-stage.*) There's some protection from the wind and snow.

Larry: Who'd have thought it? An imposter in our midst!

They all exit, Larry helping Scott/Paul.

Episode 5

Scene

Professor Yvonne Von Evian's shelter. There are scientific instruments, monitors etc around about the place, as well as skis, coats and other snow equipment. Our team enter in high spirits. Paul is wearing sunglasses.

Fay: This is it! We're here!

Helen: I can't believe we've made it, after all that's happened.

Larry: Yes, who'd have thought I'd get this far. And without any servants!

Paul: Are we here? Do you think I can take my sunglasses off?

Fay: Well, it is pretty dark in here, it's certainly not as bright as outside. I suppose you can take them off for a few minutes.

Paul: (*Taking off his sunglasses.*) Where is she then?

Larry: There's no one here!

Fay: Professor!

Helen: Yvonne! Are you here?

Larry: Maybe she's gone out to the shops!

Paul: There aren't many shops around here. I think the nearest supermarket must be, well, around 200 miles away.

Fay: (*Looking off-stage.*) I hope she's not outside, it looks like there's a snow storm on the way. And with those high winds, it's going to be a blizzard.

Larry: You know, after all the adventures we've had – the polar bear attack…

Helen: There was no polar bear, remember?

Paul: Yes, sorry about that.

Larry: We lost all our food, then all our equipment. Then we found that Swedish equipment store, which had more meatballs than IKEA. And then we discovered that Great Scott wasn't Great Scott after all, and was called Paul McSmall.

And then he got snow blindness and we had to lead him all the way…

Fay: What's your point, Larry?

Larry: You'd think she would have left us a note or something.

Paul: Well, it's not as if she knew we were coming!

Larry: No, I suppose not.

Fay: She can't have gone far. Let's make some tea while we wait.

Work out a slapstick routine around the four people trying to make the tea. One can go out and get some (fake) snow, which they drop on someone. They then get some more and so on. People can trip, people can drop tea bags or throw them at each other, the milk can be frozen… In the end they make four cups of tea and sit down.

Helen: Fay, I don't think you've actually told us what the message is that we had to bring to Professor Yvonne Von Evian. What is it that she needs to know so desperately?

Fay: (*Pulling an envelope from her pocket.*) It's here, but Chief told me not to open it.

Larry: Well, couldn't we try to open the envelope and find out?

Fay: No!

Larry: Oh come on. I bet we could reseal it and the Professor would never know!

Helen: Yes! If we steamed it open, we wouldn't tear the paper.

Paul: Go on Fay! I'm dying to know!

Larry: Go on Fay!

Fay: (*Looking doubtful before relenting.*) Oh, alright then. I'm sure she'll tell us when she reads it anyway.

They all crowd round the envelope as Fay tries to peel the corner back. Suddenly the door opens and the Professor walks in accompanied by a whoosh of fake snow. She is completely cocooned in outdoor clothing. We can barely see her face. However, the team are so

intent on opening the envelope that they don't notice. The Professor walks off stage the other side.

Fay: Did you feel a big draft then?

Larry: Sorry, I burped.

Fay, Helen and Paul: Eurgh!

They go back to the envelope. The Professor appears, this time without her coat and scarf. She notices them and walks up behind them, watching what Fay is doing. They stay like this for a moment before the Professor speaks.

Yvonne: What are you doing?

The others shout in surprise – they hadn't noticed she was there. Fay hastily reseals the envelope, hoping the Professor hasn't seen.

Fay: Professor! How good to see you!

Helen: We've come such a long way!

Paul: And learnt so much!

Larry: And eaten so many meatballs!

Yvonne: Well, it's good to see you – I've been cut off for months. My radio stopped working and I haven't been able to contact anyone. Even my satellite phone is broken.

Fay: The Chief sent us with this message. (*She hands the Professor the envelope.*)

Larry: (*As the Professor is opening the envelope.*) I hope you don't mind me asking, but you're very young to be a professor.

Paul: I was thinking that too!

Yvonne: Yes, I suppose I am! I went to university when I was really young, and so when I was ready to join the team, I was about ten years younger than everyone else. No one thought I should be part of any expeditions, as I was so young. But the Chief knew I was ready, regardless of how old I was. And here I am, doing some great research at the pole!

She finally opens the envelope and reads the letter. She smiles, nods and puts the paper back in the envelope.

Helen: What does it say?

Larry: I'm dying to know!

Paul: Come on Professor!

Fay: If you're allowed to tell us, we'd love to know. After all, we've brought it all this way.

Yvonne: Of course. The Chief needed to tell me that I was being sent a new team to help me in my work here.

Helen: (*A bit crestfallen.*) Oh, is that it?

Fay: That's not a very exciting message.

Larry: You mean we risked life and limb and Curly Wurly to deliver that?

Paul: I wonder why the Chief didn't just send the new team with the message.

Yvonne: He did.

Larry: Hang on, do you mean that there's another team on their way with the same message? Oh I could have stayed at home and got my servants to feed me cake all day long!

Yvonne: No Larry! Think about it. You are my new team!

Fay: (*Getting the idea and smiling.*) Oh!

Helen: (*Getting the idea and smiling.*) Oh!

Paul: (*Getting the idea and smiling.*) Oh!

Larry: (*Not getting the idea at all.*) Eh?

Yvonne: You're staying here – you're going to help me!

Larry: (*Getting the idea and smiling.*) Oh!

Yvonne: Now you've brought another radio, we can make contact with HQ and you can let everyone know what's happening.

Larry: But my servants! What will they do without me to look after?

Fay: They'll probably have a well-earned rest!

Helen: And I'll be able to do lots of cross-country skiing here, gathering information for the Professor's research – lots of danger and lots of excitement!

Paul: And I'll get a chance to prove what I can do!

Fay: And I'll enjoy not being in charge for a while. I might even have a nap right now!

Yvonne: Well, don't get too comfortable, there's lots to be done. But for now, let's have some food and get an early night – you deserve it!

They all laugh and go off chatting excitedly about what they're going to do.

• • • • • • • • • • • • • • • • • • • •

Service 2

Scene

The Professor's station, with the same range of equipment and scientific instruments as Episode 5. The characters come on from either side, holding clipboards/tablets, bringing in a tray of tea etc. As one character swings round some skis, another instinctively ducks. One person picks up tea and gives it to another, on their way to completing another task.

Yvonne: It's been amazing having you here. We've been working together so well, and we've only just got started!

Paul: Well, Prof, we learnt so much on our journey here and went through so much, that we became quite a team!

Helen: I made so many mistakes in the past, but being given another chance and with the help of my friends, I've done some great things! You've never made too many mistakes to be part of the expedition.

Fay: Yes, we never would have survived if you hadn't skied to the Swedish equipment store.

Larry: Mm… All those meatballs.

Fay: And we discovered that the most unlikely people can be good at many things – who would have thought Larry would have saved us all with his birthday banquet food parcel!

Larry: (*Embarrassed.*) Oh, you guys! You're never too ordinary to be part of the expedition!

Fay: And I learnt that no matter how far away something is, or how desperate the situation, you need to trust the advice you get from the people who know. You're never too near or far to stay part of the expedition.

Paul: And I learnt the most important lesson of all. That we need to work for the good of everyone and not be selfish. Thankfully, the Chief and the team forgave all the horrible things I did. You're never too bad to be part of the expedition!

Yvonne: And I've always known that you're never too young! You know, we should make a record of all of this so we remember. Why don't we make a video log?

Helen: Ooh, a vlog! Great idea Prof!

Larry: You know, I know I don't need them, but I still miss my servants. It is nice to put your feet up while someone does something for you.

Fay: We thought as much, so Paul and I made you a surprise! Go and get it Paul.

Larry: Ooh, I love surprises!

Paul and Helen go out and return with a giant highly decorated cake and a tray of tea. Paul puts the cake in front of Larry. But as Helen brings the tray in, she trips and falls against Yvonne, who pushes Fay, who nudges Paul, who accidentally pushes Larry's face into the cake. Larry eventually lifts his face up and it's covered in icing. The others looked shocked at what's happened.

Helen, Yvonne, Fay and Paul: (*All together*) Sorry, Larry.

Larry puts his fingertip into the icing on his face then licks it. He breaks into a big smile.

Larry: What could be better – a face full of cake, made by my expedition team!

He grabs a handful of cake and shoves it into his mouth. Someone hands him a towel, and they all go off together.

EXPEDITION STORE 4
OTHer resources

Strips for Working out your aims

To **attract new children** to join your Sunday groups or other children's activities.

To **develop your leaders**' gifts and experience.

To **present the gospel** to children who've never heard it.

To **provide an opportunity** for children to make an initial or further commitment to follow Jesus.

To **get to know the children** in your church.

To **help children** in your church to **grow in faith**.

To **provide a project** to encourage your church to work together.

To **establish links** with the children's families.

To encourage cooperation with other churches or groups in your area.

To **launch an ongoing children's group**, meeting midweek.

To **give parents a break** in the school holidays.

POLar EXPLORERS theme song

searching For your truth

Pete Sheath

Copyright © 2014 Scripture Union

searching for your truth POLAR EXPLORERS theme song 2

searching for your truth POLAR EXPLORERS theme song 3

Copyright © 2014 Scripture Union

Flame templates for Flame headbands

Arrow templates for Woven compass

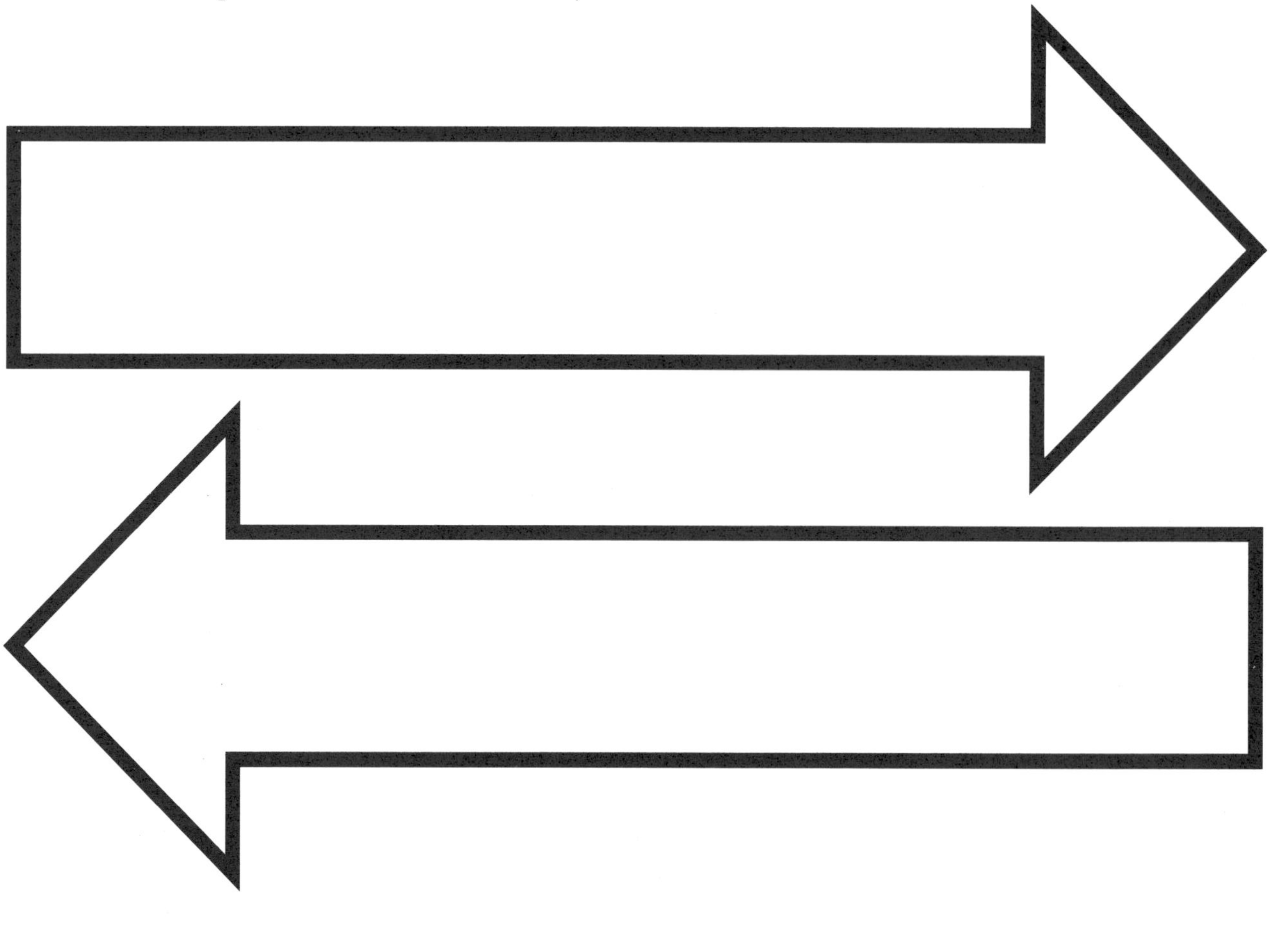

Instructions for East West game

EAST WEST game

Instruction	Explanation
North	Children run to the front of the space
East	Children run to the right wall of the space
South	Children run the back of the space
West	Children run to the left wall of the space
Spinning compass	Children spin around on the spot
Pitch a tent	Children get into groups of three and put their arms up to a centre point (as if they are the three corners of the tents)
Tunnelling	Children lie down on their fronts, on the floor, and use their arms to move forward
Fly the flag	Children mime raising a flag (pulling rope up and down)
Backpack	Children get into pairs and stand back to back
Light the fire	Children crouch down into a small ball and the jump up as high as they can (miming the camp fire starting)
Polar Explorers	Children salute and shout 'Explorer [*name*] reporting for duty'

Commands for Pass the backpack

Dance a jig

Sing 'Twinkle, twinkle little star'

Do ten star jumps

Do an impression of a chicken

Do an impression of a monkey

Sing 'Heads, shoulders, knees and toes' and do the actions

Run around the circle three times

Hop on the spot for one minute

Keep your hand on your head for one minute

Swap places with three people in the circle

Tell a joke

Say three words in another language

Checklists for Scavenger hunt

scavenger HUNT CHECKLIST

- [ ] Three different leaves
- [ ] Something red
- [ ] Something beginning with the letter 's'
- [ ] Something beginning with the letter 'a'
- [ ] Something with words on it
- [ ] Something pretty
- [ ] Something soft
- [ ] Something old
- [ ] Something with stripes on it
- [ ] Something round
- [ ] Something sparkly

scavenger HUNT CHECKLIST

- [ ] Three different leaves
- [ ] Something red
- [ ] Something beginning with the letter 's'
- [ ] Something beginning with the letter 'a'
- [ ] Something with words on it
- [ ] Something pretty
- [ ] Something soft
- [ ] Something old
- [ ] Something with stripes on it
- [ ] Something round
- [ ] Something sparkly

FOLLOW-UP ACTIVITIES
Keep on exploring

Follow-up ideas

During your holiday club week, you will more than likely make contact with children and families who have little or no regular contact with church. At **Polar Explorers** the children will have heard truths from the Bible, built positive relationships with your team and enjoyed being in community. It's a long time to wait until you do it all again next year! The following ideas aim to enable you to continue the important work you have begun and begin to disciple the children on a more regular basis, turning your holiday club ministry into a year-round ministry to children who may be currently outside the reach of your church.

Family ministry

It is vital to remember that children are part of families (of all shapes and sizes) and that mission to the whole family is an essential part of passing on the stories and love of Jesus.

With a view to reaching the whole family, start inviting them to belong to the community, through events and in developing relationships. Once good relationships have been established, personal faith may be shared. This might take a long time to develop, but long-term commitment to children and families is essential. The ideas outlined below and those at www.exploretogether.org will provide you with some starting points for continuing the work with the children and for connecting with whole families.

Top Tips on Growing faith with families is full of helpful advice if you're looking to start a family ministry.

Afternoon/evening activities

The **Polar Explorers** daily outlines provide enough material for one session: morning or afternoon. However, depending on the energy levels of your team and financial resources of your children/families/ church, the holiday club lends itself to an optional extended programme.

It is a good idea to include some events in your club for families to attend all together. During your holiday club, you could add trips, picnics or visits to nearby attractions after the club session or at the weekend. Or arrange a 'family fun night' with activities for all ages to do together with options you didn't have time to try out during the club. This will give you a chance to meet and get to know the families of children who are coming to **Polar Explorers**. Involve the whole church to organise food or run activities. Events like these can be used to extend the **Polar Explorers** theme over the whole summer holidays, if that's when you are running your club, with afternoon or evening events taking place in the weeks following the club.

Here are a few things you could try:

- **Games**: organise a family games event, using some of the games ideas from pages 74 to 76. Families could work together, or you could pair a family from your church community with one new to the church, to help build relationships.
- **Construction**: use some of the construction ideas on pages 70 to 73 to put together a family session. Choose activities that encourage family members to work together (for instance, fathers and sons). You could combine construction and games into one event.
- **Run a 'party day'** during or after the club with all sorts of activities and skill sessions, led by

members of the team. Hire a bouncy castle or ball pool. Blow giant bubbles; learn to juggle or make your own pizzas. Play giant versions of four-in-a-row, *Jenga* wooden towers or pick-up-sticks. Set out table-top games such as chess, snakes and ladders and dominoes. Run a 'beetle drive'.

- **Treasure hunt**: set up a large-scale treasure hunt for families or small teams to follow. With intergenerational teams, you could expand this beyond your building into the local area with riddles to solve or clues linked to the geographical area.
- **Family barbecue**: these events are always popular and can be quite simple to run. Alongside the food, you could run games or construction, or a family quiz which could include questions about the **POLar EXPLOrers** Bible stories.
- **Big screen events**: explore what recent or not-so-recent children's films you could show, which may, or may not have a specifically Christian content. Provide popcorn and all the other features of a trip to the cinema. (Remember that you need the correct licence for the public showing of a film.)
- **Day out**: arrange a trip to an attraction, such as a theme park, child-friendly museum, water park, play centre or activity centre. (Fundraise beforehand, so you can offer this to all the families connected to your club.)

These simple ideas can appear groundbreaking to those who are unfamiliar with your church. Run in conjunction with the club, they can involve more members of the church community, introduce the church to people with little or no previous contact, in a relaxed atmosphere, and start to build positive relationships.

Have a sleepover

A popular idea to enhance the contact and maintain the relationships with the children who attend is to have a sleepover. You could do this (maybe with some fresh team!) on the last night of the club, perhaps after a family BBQ or, if you prefer, some months later when you could roll a Saturday night sleepover into a morning service and so invite and include those who were part of the holiday club but are not regular church attendees.

Family reunion evening

A family reunion event, which could be held in a half-term school break following **POLar EXPLOrers**, allows children to revisit the ideas and themes of the club and to show their families the kinds of things they were involved in. Try to have as many of the **POLar EXPLOrers** team available as you can, as this will help children maintain the relationships they had at the club.

Here is a suggested programme:

Do you copy?

As the children arrive, they should go to their team HQs to catch up with each other. Play a game where you throw a dice and then talk about a specific topic assigned to the number you throw. Topics could include 'What I remember about **POLar EXPLOrers**', 'What I did for the rest of my holidays' or 'What I like best about school'.

Meanwhile, parents could either join in with the groups or have a drink in a café area, where photographs and pieces of artwork from the club are displayed. Make this environment as warm and welcoming as possible and ensure that a number of team members are available to talk to parents and welcome them as they arrive.

Base camp

Sing the **POLar EXPLOrers** song and have a *Basic training* race. Explain the stories and themes of each day in the club. You could show the most popular DVD story from the club, too.

Games

Play some of the most popular games from **POLar EXPLOrers**; you could even encourage the parents to take part!

Song and prayer

Choose a favourite song from the week to sing together, and then end with a prayer. Thank the parents for sending their children to the club. Provide information about other up-and-coming events to be held at church.

Food

Share a simple meal together.

Midweek clubs

An ideal way to maintain contact with children is to hold a midweek club at your church or local primary school. Scripture Union publishes *eye level* resources, aimed at midweek clubs for primary age children, especially those with no church background. Go to www.scriptureunion.org.uk/2368.id and choose any *eye level* club as a follow-up to **POLar EXPLorers**.

So, Why God?, another *eye level* club, is suitable if you have children who are interested in knowing more about being a Christian. It takes questions children ask about following Jesus and helps them to come up with an answer. It also leads children in a sensitive way through the process of becoming a Christian. (See the inside front cover for details of *So, Why God?*)

After-school activities

Many schools run after-school activities, so a weekly **POLar EXPLorers** club could become a fantastic follow-up to the holiday club, engaging with the children where they are already at – in school. In negotiation with the head teacher and key members of staff, the club would be able to provide creative art workshops for children, including the telling of a Bible story and some opportunity for discussion. This will work best in small groups of no more than 12 children.

POLar EXPLorers days

Day events held throughout the year are good to maintain contact with holiday club children. These are effective when they coincide with a special time of the year: harvest, alternative Halloween, Christmas, new year, Valentine's Day, Easter.

Here is a suggested programme:

- Registration and *Do you copy?*
- *Base camp* (with story, teaching, songs, games and so on)
- Games
- Break
- Small-group Bible exploration
- Lunch
- Construction
- Break
- *Expedition debrief* (songs, *Learn and remember* verse, recap on story, interview)
- Team time for interactive prayer and response time

It might also be possible to run additional **POLar EXPLorers** days when the local school has an in-service training day. Gathering a team may be more difficult as many will be at work, but it can be of real service to the community and parents who will need to be at work themselves.

Family days

The programme above need not be limited to children. There is something spiritual about families sharing and learning together. Ability is not an issue, and the children will enjoy helping other adults in activities with which they are comfortable. What about holding a **POLar EXPLorers** day where you invite the family members of the children who attended the holiday club? (Parents, siblings, grandparents, aunts/uncles, godparents are all welcome!)

X:site

X:site is a children's event for 7- to 11-year-olds. Each event takes place every two months in towns, cities or whole areas and combines silly games, live music, videos, creative prayer, craft, drama, Bible stories and lots more so that everyone can learn about Jesus and have fun at the same time!

X:site is a great way to encourage children in your church by bringing them together with other children in their community – they will have such a good time that they will want to invite their friends to come too. **X:site** is organised in each area by a partnership of local churches; Scripture Union is really keen to see more **X:site** events happening around the country. With your help there could be one near you.

Check out the website http://www.xsiteuk.org/ and, if you want to get involved, get in touch with us. We would really love to hear from you!